T0122160

By This My FATHER *is* GLORIFIED . . .

Lessons Learned in the Vineyard John 15

JO HINDS

WESTBOW
P R E S S®
A DIVISION OF THOMAS NELSON
& ZONDERVAN

Unless otherwise stated, scripture quotations taken from the New American Standard Bible® (NASB), Copyright © 1960, 1962, 1963, 1968, 1971, 1972, 1973, 1975, 1977, 1995 by The Lockman Foundation Used by permission. www.Lockman.org

Scripture taken from the King James Version of the Bible.

Scripture quotations marked MSG are taken from THE MESSAGE, copyright © 1993, 1994, 1995, 1996, 2000, 2001, 2002 by Eugene H. Peterson. Used by permission of NavPress. All rights reserved. Represented by Tyndale House Publishers, Inc.

WestBow Press books may be ordered through booksellers or by contacting:

WestBow Press
A Division of Thomas Nelson & Zondervan
1663 Liberty Drive
Bloomington, IN 47403
www.westbowpress.com
1 (866) 928-1240

ISBN: 978-1-9736-2647-3 (sc)
ISBN: 978-1-9736-2648-0 (hc)
ISBN: 978-1-9736-2646-6 (e)

Library of Congress Control Number: 2018904773

Print information available on the last page.

WestBow Press rev. date: 04/21/2018

Dedication and Acknowledgements

No one has ever given me more freedom to grow in Christ than my husband, Hilaire Hinds. Throughout our marriage, he has encouraged me to follow God with abandonment. Thanks also to friends who listened while I sorted out truth from deception, and encouraged me to finish this project: Dave and Debby Tripp, Don and Cheri Wilson, Dale Bromell, Katy Libke, Ronni Simmons, and my dear cousin Linda Davis who has always encouraged me to write.

Along the way many incidents, good and bad, have made me who I am today. Only a God who loves me as I am could have brought me to today – in love with Him, and more thankful for His grace every day.

CONTENTS

INTRODUCTION

"...that I may know Him and the power of His resurrection
and the fellowship of His sufferings, being conformed to His death;
in order that I may attain to the resurrection from the dead."
Philippians 3:10-11

John, Chapter 15, is a vast storehouse of spiritual treasure. Jesus explains complex spiritual principles using this word picture: "I am the vine; you are the branches...". John 15:5a The hearers of Jesus' teachings already understood their daily dependence on the vineyard for essential foods. For Jesus' followers, the vineyard was a daily living reminder of God's love, and Godly living.This book is part of my personal longing to plumb the depths of the lingering question, "I know you Lord, but who are You? I know you as my Savior and King; I want to know you as my friend."

Every time Jesus spoke, he spoke to the hearts of the people as well as their intellect. He was not particularly interested in *educating...* He sought to *transform* his listeners. He knew that no amount of information could change a person unless the inner core –the heart – was literally changed. He most desired to reach those who came like little children... those still capable of simple trust, selfless generosity, and hearts willing to learn. First, He wants an intimate relationship with his children. Then, He wants us to have deep relationships with our brothers and sisters in the faith that will demonstrate the love of God, and will disciple by word and deed.

As you study this word picture and how I believe it applies to the present body of Christ, I pray that your heart will be open to Christ as your friend *in all things*, because He is the center and focus of *all* things.

The Vineyard

Jesus said: "I am the true vine,
and My Father is the Vinedresser."
John 15:1

The vineyard is a beautiful sight. The rows of foliage are lush and the fruit is fragrant when harvest time is near. Sunlight plays on the leaves; they shimmer as slight breezes waft among the rows. Everything is orderly and clean. The terraced hillside rows grow out of the ground like natural outcroppings. Each vine has its own place, and its own purpose.

The Vinedresser and His appointed workers treat each vine for any sickness that might keep it from producing good fruit. They water at the right time, remove weeds, and carefully shade the fruit until the end of the season. Then, they hedge the vines so the fruit will receive the exact amount of sunlight it needs to finish maturing. When the grapes have ripened to sweet perfection, the Vinedresser says, "Go," and His workers hurry to harvest the fruit

It is hard to imagine what the countryside looked like before the vines took root, because they seem to fit so naturally - as if they had always been there. That is not the case, though. At one time, the vineyard was barren. The hillsides were steep and dangerously hard to climb. Thistles and weeds flourished.

Before planting vines, the Vinedresser makes many important decisions. The climate, the location, and the growing conditions determine the vine's ability to root and prosper. A step-by-step transformation takes place. Doing everything in the correct order is vital to the growth of young vines. The Vinedresser plans before he plants.

Strong young shoots grafted onto mature, healthy, disease-resistant rootstock ensures vigorous growth. Preparing the ground to receive disease-resistant rootstock is the first step. Workers remove the thick brush, weeds, and other obstacles that would prevent deep rooting. Next, hillsides are terraced. Dry-stacked stone walls keep the terraces from falling away during the rainy season. And finally, deep tilling allows young vines to grow a long *taproot* (the primary root that grows straight down into the ground and anchors the plant in place). After the vineyard is fully prepared, and the weather is perfect, the Vinedresser tells His workers to plant the vines.

The Vinedresser watches over the vineyard day and night from His high tower in the center of the vineyard. His appointed workers protect the vines with the hope that none will be lost. It is the Vinedresser's desire that each vine will grow to maturity, and effortlessly produce vast quantities of sweet fruit. The vineyard is a beautiful picture of the Body of Christ.

In that day,
"A vineyard of wine, sing of it!
I, the LORD, am its keeper;
I water it every moment.
So that no one will damage it, I guard it night and day.
I have no wrath.
Should someone give Me briars
and thorns in battle,
Then I would step on them.
I would burn them completely.
Or let him rely on My protection,
Let him make peace with Me.
Let him make peace with Me.
In the days to come Jacob will take root,
Israel will blossom and sprout;
And they will fill the whole world with fruit."

Isaiah 27:2-6

The Vinedresser
is the Strong Tower

"The name of the LORD is a strong tower:
the righteous runneth into it, and is safe."
Proverbs 18:10 kjv

There is a tower in the middle of the vineyard. From this vantage point, the Vinedresser can see everything happening in His vineyard. He also sees any enemy that comes in covertly. His keen eye sees signs of sickness before it spreads, and He can tell which vines need special attention. He watches every vine individually, and all of the vines collectively, from His high tower. He knows what every vine needs. When God planted me in His vineyard, He removed the veil over my eyes so I could clearly see the contrast of my old life and my new life in Christ. He sends His laborers to help if I lack any good thing. He is always watching; He guards me with unfailing devotion. I am precious to Him.

Thorns, thistles and weeds rambled on the ground of my life before I became part of God's vineyard, but the ground into which God planted me had no brambles. *He made a way through the death and resurrection of His own son, to remove the weeds from my life.* When I asked God to forgive my sin, He washed me clean and grafted me into His vineyard. Every vine in the vineyard of God begins in this same way. Each one is the planting of the LORD. The Vinedresser provides care and protection for each of them.

All young vines are weak. They do not have a deep taproot in the beginning. I remember many things about the early years of my walk with the LORD. I was always thirsty, and the early seasons produced weak fruit. He has spent many years training me, and forming me into His image. I know that I am still growing. He always knows what is best for me... even when I do not understand His purposes.

When I look back at all of my life experiences, I find each of them had a purpose. The smallest details come flooding back as I think through the years, and I see how the good and the bad have woven together. I know that my redeemer lives, and He loves me. I am at peace.

God knew the right location for me in His vineyard. He knew which vines to plant around me. He knew, before I ever bore any fruit, what kind of fruit I would bear – that it would mellow and become more complex as I aged. He always knows exactly what kind of pruning method works to cause me to bear the best fruit. When dangers lurk, He protects me. He is the strong tower in the vineyard. He is at the very center of the vineyard and my life. I can truly say,

> "LORD, I have loved the habitation of thy house,
> and the place where thine honour dwelleth."
> Psalm 26:8 kjv

The LORD is the Strong Tower

The Vinedresser's Presence

"I am the Rose of Sharon, and the lily of the valleys.
The fig tree putteth forth her green figs,
and the vines with the tender grape give a good smell.
Arise, my love, my fair one, and come away."
Song of Solomon 2:1, 13 kjv

When the Vinedresser comes into the vineyard, His presence makes Him known. His fragrance fills the vineyard as He walks through. The scent of flowers planted at the ends of the rows drives away pests that destroy the fruit; He moves among the vines. He speaks to instruct His workers, and to comfort His vines. He waits; He watches. He takes decisive action to insure the safety of the vines. He makes all final decisions about what happens in the vineyard. He is gentle. His touch sooths each vine as He examines its leaves and inspects the ripening fruit. He talks quietly; He moves with purpose and great pleasure. Great men of God through the ages have learned to know God like this.

Noah knew Him as a Savior who rescued his family when all others perished in the flood. Abraham knew Him as his provider, and believed Him when He promised future greatness for his descendants. Joseph knew Him as the one who provided wisdom when starvation was imminent in Egypt. King David expressed his knowledge of God in the Psalms, and Elijah, the prophet, knew Him as the God with whom he had a personal relationship.

The Bible tells us in I Kings chapter 19 that Elijah encountered the LORD's presence when he feared for his life. The story goes like this: Elijah challenged the prophets of Baal, and eventually destroyed them. Ahab reported what happened to his evil wife Jezebel, and she was furious. She sent a message to Elijah saying she planned to kill him. To escape, Elijah walked from Beer-Sheba to Horeb – a forty day journey, and hid in a cave. The LORD spoke to Elijah - asking him what he was doing hiding in a cave. God tested Elijah's trust by asking Elijah to leave the cave. The LORD wanted him to stand on the mountain as He passed by. Elijah knew Jezebel's men were searching for him, and he could not bring himself to leave the cave. Elijah thought the voice might be a trick. Fear gripped him so strongly he doubted his ability to know if he was hearing God's voice. What if Jezebel's soldiers were outside the cave? Elijah remained in the cave, even at the command of the LORD. Fear is a powerful weapon in Satan's arsenal. It keeps many people from fully surrendering in God's presence.

While he remained hidden, Elijah heard a wind so strong it tore the rocks apart. Then, an earthquake occurred followed by a fire. Still, Elijah remained in the cave. It was not until Elijah heard the sound of a gentle wind blowing that he knew the LORD was present, and it was safe for him to leave the cave. When he emerged from the cave, the LORD asked Elijah once again, "What are you doing here, Elijah"? (I Kings 19:8-14)

Why does the LORD ask us questions when He already knows the answer? In this case, I think the LORD wanted Elijah to admit that he was hiding because he feared Jezebel. When the LORD asked again, Elijah could have admitted that he was bound by his fear of man. Instead, Elijah claimed his zeal for the work of the LORD caused his fear. Elijah wanted God to know his present unwillingness to be obedient was caused by his good deeds in the past. What do you think?

Elijah knew God's presence, but he refused to be obedient to the voice of the LORD because his fear of man was greater than his willingness to obey. Was Elijah honest with God, and himself, about his reason for hiding? Can you think of any situation where a well-meaning person did something similar when God asked them to risk being obedient? After reading this story, can you tell that Elijah, in spite of his fears, knew God? How do you know?

God loves us. When He is present we are safe. We can risk surrendering completely because He is not in the fearsome noises, earthquakes, fires that burn, or any other thing that strikes fear in our hearts. There is no wrath in Him toward His people. He is fully for us, and not against us. His love comes gently. The LORD showed Elijah that he did not need to be afraid of His presence. He came to Elijah tenderly, quietly, gently. He will do that for you, too.

Risk worshipping with all your heart. Bow before Him. Adore Him. Let His sweet presence envelope you. You will never regret being obedient when He asks you to obey, *but you must know Him*. Until you know that you know Him, always verify that the voice you are listening to is indeed the voice of God. Then, obedience will no longer be a risk – it will be a pleasure.

Vines in God's vineyard know Him as a gentle blowing of the wind, a sweet fragrance – a quiet voice filled with love. The vines bow to Him as He passes by. Have you experienced God in this way? The vines tremble in His awesome presence, but they are, at the same time, content and at peace. Can you tell the difference between the voice in your mind, and the voice of God? May God interrupt your busy life any time He wants to speak? Does He need to shout to get your attention? Is there a quiet time when He can come with a still, small voice and say, "walk this way"?

Do you want to know the answer – the Biblical answer - when God speaks to you? He may not speak in an audible voice, but you will know the truth if you *actively listen*. Sometimes His voice is a subtle impression felt in your spirit. Always test what you hear. What He says will agree with known Biblical doctrine and truth. When you listen carefully, He will teach you. His Holy Spirit is the revealer of all truth. (John 14:26)

Do you listen for His voice? Some of the time; only on Sunday morning during the worship service; once in a while; never? The most important question to ask is this: does *fear* hold you back from believing that God wants a personal relationship with you?

Do you meditate upon His word often during your day? Do you ask the Holy Spirit to explain things to you? He will, if you ask Him. Answers often come during times of prolonged worship – quiet, focused worship - and times of prayer. God waits until we *listen*. If you talk through your entire prayer time, at some point stop talking, and wait upon Him.

In many churches today, a Christian church service is more like a rock concert, or new age meditation than an opportunity to meet God face to face in the Holy of Holies. Entertaining the troops with a raucous secularly patterned rock concert, or the drone of new age music that repetitively creates a mantra of meditation does not provide an entrance into God's presence. These practices grieve the Holy Spirit, and He withdraws. When true worship is lacking in a congregation, those who have experienced it elsewhere sense the grieving of the Holy Spirit, and their hearts break. When the Holy Spirit withdraws, the only thing left to hold a stagnant or dying congregation together is community service, and behavior based on law instead of grace.

Worship occurs in church services, and any time during the day, when you stop to think of Him, and draw near with gratitude in your heart. It is during times of worship that the Holy Spirit flows like a still small voice, or breeze in the vineyard. The vines yield to Him, and dance in the breeze. They move spontaneously to follow His lead. How do you define worship? Is it solely a time for honoring God – Father, Son, and Holy Spirit, or something else?

Two disciples met Jesus on the road to Emmaus. Jesus spoke to them, "beginning with Moses and with all the prophets, He explained to them the things concerning Himself in all the scriptures." (Luke 24:27) Five books of the Bible explain the purpose of the tabernacle: Exodus, Leviticus, Numbers, Deuteronomy, and Hebrews. The tabernacle is a rich source of prophetic information. It also reveals a pattern for living. Read Hebrews chapter nine.

The Jewish tabernacle had an outer court, an inner court, and a Holy of Holies. It shows us how to worship. One passes through the *outer court* to the *inner court* by passing by the *brazen altar* where the blood sacrifices occurred (Jesus shed His blood for us). We enter the *outer court* with thanksgiving and praise – expressing our gratitude for what God has done for us through our Savior's sacrifice.

As we pass through the *inner court*, we walk by the *candlestick*, (Jesus is the light of the world); the *shew bread*, (Jesus is the bread of life); and *the altar of incense*, (our place of prayer). Finally, we enter into the Holy of Holies. The tabernacle had a thick curtain separating the *inner court* from the most sacred of all places, the *Holy of Holies*. Only a priest could go into the Holy of Holies, and then once a year to bring the blood of the sacrifice at Passover. There is no longer a curtain separating us from God because Jesus opened up this most sacred location by the shedding of His blood. We are now priests in the spiritual temple of God, and we do not need to wait; we can come to God any day of the year. (Revelation 5:10). In the Holy of Holies, we come face to face with our LORD. (Hebrews 10:19-22).

Is it possible to enter His gates with thanksgiving, and His courts with praise, and then not pass through the inner court to the Holy of Holies? Yes, it is. Most churches, in my experience, do just that. Have you ever been in a worship service that led you into the Holy of Holies? Once you experience His presence in the Holy of Holies, no other form of worship will fully satisfy that longing in your soul.

Worship is not a time for singing about our own wants, needs, or desires. *If the songs focus on me… my desires, likes or wants… it is not worship.* Worship focuses on God alone. During the praise portion of praise and worship, we *acknowledge our thanksgiving*, but during worship, everything *acknowledges Him alone*.

Who is called to lead worship? A *worship leader* does not focus on his/ her audience as an entertainer does. A worship leader understands that his/ her function is to lead the congregation from the outer court, through the inner court, and into the Holy of Holies. The worship leader must choose songs that will take the people to meet with God. It is a progression from praise to worship through music (Hebrews 4:16).

A worship leader must sense the presence of the Spirit, and flow with what he/she is hearing/sensing in the Holy Spirit. Sometimes people enter in quickly, and sometimes it takes longer. Worship ebbs and flows. A worship leader that sings like a lark, but does not comprehend the ways of the Spirit cannot take a congregation into the Holy of Holies. At the entrance to the Holy of Holies, the worship leader ebbs the music into silence, and waits while God reveals His presence through the Holy Spirit.

The gifts of the Spirit flow during this time, and God's still small voice is heard by individuals. God's quiet voice cannot be heard when the environment is filled with noise. The worship leader watches and waits upon the Lord – continually asking the Holy Spirit when to take the people in, and when to bring them out again. When we worship together the body is united, and the cry of every heart is, "You are LORD." This is unity.

This is when God convicts hearts of sin, and mends hearts with His mercy and grace… things only God can do. It is in the habitation of our hearts that God meets with us. Only when renewed in the spirit of our minds through the *transformation of our hearts* can we put on the new self that is in the likeness of God. (I Corinthians 2:12)

The Lord may come as an impression in the emotions, as words in your mind, a sense of something you need to do… it is difficult to explain, but every person He touches knows when He is genuinely present. His peace fills the room, and hearts begin to soften. His love flows like a warm liquid. It is impossible to describe adequately, but *once He touches you, you will never be the same* (Colossians 3:15-17).

Are you listening for the "sound of a gentle blowing? What do you think God would say to you, if you were to listen for that still, small voice? Do you *fear* that silence? Listen anyway. He is your sovereign King. When you know His presence, you know Him.

Listen.
Hear Him speak.
Enjoy being with Him.
Obey.
His sweet fragrance in the vineyard means
He is near.

"There is no fear in love;
but perfect love casteth out fear:
because fear hath torment.
He that feareth
is not made perfect in love.
We love Him,
because
He first loved us."

I John 4:18-19 kjv

The Branches Reflect His Light and His Glory

"The sun shall be no more thy light by day;
neither for brightness shall the moon give light unto thee;
but the Lord shall be unto thee an everlasting light,
and thy God thy glory."
Isaiah 60:19 kjv

The sun shines; the wind blows; light dances through the vineyard. The leaves do not see the wind, but they yield to its touch. Light and shadows change as each leaf dances in the breeze. When the sun shines, it falls on everything. It is true that bright sunlight creates dark shadows. When the light of Christ shines out of our hearts, those who experience our presence become more aware of any darkness present in their own lives (Matthew 5:14-16).

When we allow God to transform our lives, He makes His presence known through us in the world. We often think evangelism has to be a script of Biblical language spoken by rote to a lost world, but it is often the little things – ordinary kindness that truly evangelizes. Hurting people want someone to care.

Many years ago, my husband was unemployed because of a recession in the building industry. He sold building materials for a company in Eugene, Oregon. The only job he could find was in California. After we moved to Livermore, California, the recession slowly crept south. Seven months after we moved, the company that hired him closed. We were stranded financially.

Fortunately, we had many new Christian friends. That period in our lives taught us how to trust God with everything. One day while I was home alone, the doorbell rang. By the time I opened the door whoever was there had left, but I found a bag of groceries on the doorstep. I was grateful for this gift of love, but I would have given every morsel in that bag for the hug that could have gone with it. I learned an incredibly valuable lesson that day. Nothing is more important than a human touch. No amount of material assistance can replace personal relationships. We need one another. As times become more difficult in our culture, personal relationships, for many Christians will be the difference between fighting the good fight successfully, and destruction by deception.

Vines stay together. They surround one another, and help one another. Vines shield one another in the presence of strong winds. Through warm sunny days and the hardships of winter, the vines remain planted together.

Anyone who has had the pleasure of spending time in a wooded park on a sunny day knows the feelings evoked by bright sunlight, warm breezes, and dancing shadows. The movement of the leaves and the warmth of the sun bring comfort and well-being. When the gentle winds of the Holy Spirit come through the vineyard, the branches know Him and respond. They move with Him, and they delight in His touch. The world outside His vineyard holds no lasting pleasure for these branches. They are satisfied to be with Him (John 3:8).

The most powerful expression of worship is time with God alone. It is intimate, but sometimes we hesitate because we know our own frailties. We know He can lay us bare without speaking a word if we have sinned against Him, but He is not the one who condemns us. We condemn ourselves. We understand true reverential fear of God only as He reveals Himself to each of us personally. We have His assurance that we are safe with Him. His peace is always with us (John 14:27).

All of our fears about inadequacy, unrepentant sin and imperfection are already known by Him. He sees none of them after we acknowledge them, and ask Him for forgiveness.

We cannot hide.

Run to Him.

Yield to Him in humility
and
Live in the light
of
His Glory

Preparing the Ground

"...We eagerly wait for a Savior, the Lord Jesus Christ;
who will transform the body of our humble state
into conformity with the body of His Glory,
by the exertion of the power that He has
even to subject all things to Himself."
Philippians 3:20-21

Consider the environment, or culture, in a vineyard. When it is right, the vines flourish. Vines require neutral or slightly acidic soil. Volcanic ground is ideal. Volcanic ground is high in nutrients and has excellent drainage, but vines will also grow in soil amended to make good drainage possible. In many parts of the world vines grow on steep, terraced hillsides, but vines grow equally well on level ground. All vines that flourish (not just survive) require a *continual flow of water, bright light, consistent feeding,* and *protection from disease.*

Vines produce fruit sooner and yields are larger when they have perfect growing conditions, but they can survive difficult conditions if necessary. However, they survive very dry conditions and hot climates only if they have a deep enough root system. This also describes congregations of believers.

Some congregations are dry. A dry place is one where the most important thing is simply doing one's moral duty by attending Church services every Sunday. Some congregations have a hot culture – a culture filled with controversy, the works of the flesh, and emotional drama instead of peace. A vineyard with abundant good quality fruit has adequate water (the word of God is preached), deep roots (the entire congregation prays together often), and a peaceful environment (God's love flows through the congregation).

We are the planting of the LORD. This prophetic statement tells us what the right culture in a congregation looks like:

"The Spirit of the Lord GOD *is* upon me; because the LORD hath anointed me to preach good tidings unto the meek; he hath sent me to bind up the brokenhearted, to proclaim liberty to the captives, and the opening of the prison to *them that are* bound; To proclaim the acceptable year of the LORD, and the day of vengeance of our God; to comfort all that mourn; To appoint unto them that mourn in Zion, to give unto them beauty for ashes, the oil of joy for mourning, the garment of praise for the spirit of heaviness; that they might be called trees of righteousness, the planting of the LORD, that he might be glorified. And they shall build the old wastes, they shall raise up the former desolations, and they shall repair the waste cities, the desolations of many generations. And strangers shall stand and feed your flocks, and the sons of the alien *shall be* your plowmen and your vinedressers." Isaiah 61:1-5 kjv

Christ has promised to complete the work He began in us, but many things can keep us from tapping into the depths of God so that can happen. Think about all the obstacles you have encountered. Are you tenacious – refusing to give up, courageous, choosing to go God's way no matter what, and persevering to the end? Do you know if you lack any of the qualities that will help you escape corruption? His promises, when known and believed make it possible for us to become participants in His own nature.

The death and resurrection of Jesus has allowed us to escape the world system that is completely corrupt in its very nature, and we have a personal relationship with the God who created the entire universe (II Peter 1:4-8). Consider what that means. What is it like having a personal relationship with the One who, literally, created the universe? I find it difficult to fully grasp, and completely amazing.

It is during the hard times when we most earnestly seek Him for answers. We are never alone when life brings injustice. God draws near to tell us what He requires to resolve conflict. Often we must yield something we want to keep: Our pride, our right to remain unchanged, control over our own destiny, anger, or other fleshly desires.

There are always choices between newness of life, and stagnation of personal growth in Christ. What do you choose? Many times, the best choice is the one we do not want to make, but when understood in hindsight, it brings joy. What causes a branch to willfully continue down sinful paths?

"He hath shewed thee, O man, what is good; and what doth the LORD require of thee, but to do justly, and to love mercy, and to walk humbly with thy God?" Micah 6:8 kjv

Sporadic watering causes roots to spread shallowly and horizontally in an attempt to find water. Roots entangle themselves in the root systems of vines nearby. The fruit that grows on these vines is hard, small, and bitter. It is good for nothing. When desperate, thirsty vines will grasp at the water of the vines around them instead of putting down a deep taproot. Once this happens, the vines are in peril of death during the first harsh winter. Because there is no depth, the roots freeze, and the vine dies. A deep taproot is vital to the survival of every vine. Can you relate this to the culture in a congregation of believers? What does the life of a shallowly watered believer look like? Now imagine that in an entire congregation. Based on your observations, how important is it to sanctify and cleanse the church through the washing of water by the word? (Ephesians 5:26 kjv)

When growing conditions are poor, vines wilt easily. When the Holy Spirit is truly present, the water of the word flows continually. Workers in the vineyard are responsible for tending the needs of the vines. If leadership fails to equip the saints, the Vinedresser Himself will intervene with the life-giving sustenance needed for growth, but pastors and elders must be aware that God holds them responsible for failing to fulfill their calling if they do not teach the word of God systematically. Part of discipleship is training in personal integrity, and knowing what that commitment involves comes through learning the word of God.

Yes, each person does their own study at home, but teaching that is common to the entire group brings unity. This unity, in turn, protects the congregation as a whole.

The soil: Vines cannot grow a deep taproot when *hardpan* is present. Hardpan is a thick layer of dense clay soil usually found a foot or so below the surface. It does not allow water, or taproots, to penetrate deeply. Vines planted in untilled land with a thick layer of hardpan look healthy, but they are not. The ground must be "ripped" before planting.

This kind of deep tilling breaks up hardpan. Organic matter worked deep into the soil keeps hardpan from re-forming. *Amending* hardpan ensures that a vine can grow a deep taproot and acquire the water needed to survive. We must allow God to "till" our hearts. Untilled hardness of heart causes bitterness. With bitterness comes the inability to accept truth and act on it.

Alkaline soil is "sweet soil." It has a high concentration of *mineral salts* (Calcium Carbonate). This is not the salt that heightens the flavor of our food. Mineral salts leach out of the ground and form a thick crust on the surface. High concentrations of mineral salt burns the vines. Do you find it interesting that too much "sweetness" burns the vines?

God wants personal relationships to develop so there is accountability for every member of the congregation. The Bible says we are to confess our sins to one another. God wants it to be safe for people to admit they need help. People need to know there will not be back-biting, gossip, judgment, or shunning if they admit their faults.

When Pastors and teachers do not address sin, the flames of eternal hell begin to lick at the heels of those sitting in the congregation who think it is acceptable to willfully sin with impunity. Love does not pretend all is well when there is blatant sin exposed in the Christian community. A pretense of external goodness does not hide a black heart from God. God wants our speech seasoned with salt that is *savory*, not *sweet*.

Do not reject the deep tilling of the Lord.
When He tills,
He is saying, "I love you."

Rose of Sharon

Staking

"If anyone does not abide in Me, he is thrown
away as a branch, and dries up;
and they gather them, and cast them into the fire, and they are burned.
If you abide in Me, and My words abide in you,
ask whatever you wish, and it shall be done for you."
John 15:6-7

Young vines are planted at the base of a post to which they are permanently tied. The Vinedresser plants each of us at the base of the cross of Jesus Christ. The cross brings life in the same way that the taproot brings water through the vine to the branches (Colossian 2:6-7).

To remain alive, a vine must remain planted. Uprooting brings immediate death. Our eternal life is centered and focused on the death and resurrection of Jesus. He was physically killed, but the Spirit within His physical body did not die. A well-known television evangelist said Jesus had to die spiritually, and be 'born-again' to be like us in all things. This is impossible, because God is an eternal spirit. When Jesus died, He went into hell and took captivity captive. Now He holds the keys to death and hades, and He is the anchor of our souls (Revelation 1:18, Hebrews 6:19).

I once heard a preacher say, "We must get past the cross so we can get on with our lives." Sadly, that man did not understand that the death and resurrection of Jesus is more than an event in history. Christ, His death and resurrection, are at the very core of our faith, and the cross is the place where every vine is permanently planted. The apostle Paul, who understood the power of the cross, said, "I die daily" (I Corinthians 15:31).

Jesus said to His disciples,

"And He summoned the crowd with His disciples, and said to them, 'If anyone wishes to come after Me, he must first deny himself, and take up his cross, and follow Me.'" Mark 8:34, Matthew 16:24, Luke 9:23

Rising to newness of life without dying is not possible. Only the dead are raised. We must live a crucified life. When Jesus died on the cross, He made a way of escape from the law of sin and death. Our part, and responsibility, is to die to self. This is living a crucified life.

For us, the fellowship of His sufferings is choosing to crucify the works of the flesh. The body of Christ rarely talks about this vital part of Christian living. Choosing to be dead to sin, and the sins others commit against us, is the means by which transformation of the heart occurs. Any other way is in the flesh and does not lead to spiritual transformation. When you choose to crucify the flesh, you choose life.

"For the word of the cross is to them that perish foolishness; but unto us which are saved it is the power of God." I Corinthians 1:18 kjv

We cannot move away from the cross. We are, literally, dependent upon the working of the cross in our lives. It is what forms our character, and makes it possible for us to bear good fruit that remains in our lives. The fruit of our lives is the power of God that draws others to Him.

"For to be carnally minded is death, but to be spiritually minded is life and peace." Romans 8:6kjv

It is said, "We are saved, we are being saved, and we will be saved." This sounds logical, but it is not correct. God is not *I was*, *I am*, and *I will be*. He is I AM (Exodus 3:14). While it is true that we continue to grow in faith, *salvation* is not a life-long process of self-improvement. *All of faith* is dependent on the belief that at the moment of salvation we are *complete in Christ* (Hebrews 10:10-14). Faith believes Christ won the victory over the law of sin and dead, and He has set us free by cancelling out the certificate of debt written against us. We are set apart unto God (sanctified) at the moment of salvation. We continue to grow in the grace of God as we continually commit everything to Him, and we allow Him to change us into His image (II Corinthians 3:18).

In the time of Christ, any person found guilty of a crime not worthy of death was placed in a cell. On the post next to the cell door, the guard placed a certificate of debt that stated how much time the person had to spend in prison. At the end of the sentence, the guard removed the certificate of debt, and opened the cell door. Paul tells us that Jesus nailed that certificate to the cross, and set us free (Colossians 2:12-15).

In Christ, we have all we need to live a Godly life. We believe by faith that we are set apart unto God (sanctified) as a Holy people. Any situation that tests this offers us a choice: to believe by faith, or by sight. We fight the good fight *of faith*. Christ has already supplied all of your needs (Ephesians 3:16-19).

There are countless obstacles, deceptions, enticements, and tragedies along the way, but only those who continue believing that Christ is sufficient will survive the perils of this world. We walk in the salvation we have *already* received. We walk in the sanctification with which we are already sanctified. The basis for a life of faith is this: you *believe in Christ*, and you believe that you have received *before* you see. Faith must have an object. We do not have faith in our own faith, we have faith *in Christ*.

I suffer daily from chronic pain. I have asked God to heal me, and I know He will. I need a miracle. I have been told on many occasions, "If *you* have enough faith, you will be healed." I instantly feel condemned. How much faith do I need? How do I acquire it? Can I buy it? Do I apply it to my body, or what? My mind reels with questions. Saying that I need 'enough' faith implies that faith is an *object* that can be measured. *If I acquire enough faith means it's up to me* – I can heal myself if *I* acquire enough. My faith is in Christ; He is my healer. How much salvation is enough? Put it this way: "If you have enough belief in Christ…" That sounds ridiculous to me. The truth is Christ has already done everything that needs to be done. I believe *He* will heal me, and I trust *Him* to do it. (Hebrews 10:38-39)

Do I believe in continually asking God to heal me? Yes. We know that He took our sickness upon the cross as well as our sin (Matthew 8:17). I also believe that when someone is not healed immediately, it is not because they have in some way failed. God has perfect timing, and He is sovereign in all things.

"What shall we say then: there is no injustice with God, is there? May it never be! For He says to Moses, I will have mercy on whom I have mercy, and I will have compassion on whom I have compassion. So then it does not depend on the man who wills or the man who runs, but on God who has mercy." Romans 9:14-16

I had a problem with my back that lasted several years. I continued to ask God to heal me during that time, and I asked others to pray for me. On the day when the surgery was going to happen, I went to the hospital. The doctor requested one more MRI to see if everything looked like it had two months before. I was fully prepped for surgery when the doctor came in. He put the MRI up on the light board. He said, "I can't do surgery on you, because the problem is no longer there." He pointed it out on the MRI. Then he said, "You can get dressed and go home." The pain had vanished. I had received a miracle from the Lord. I told everyone I saw from the nurses at the desk to strangers in the elevator, and on my way out the door (Matthew 8:16-17). Fighting the good fight means we continue to believe God has supplied all of our needs regardless of the circumstances. Continue to believe by faith *in Him*.

I have learned many lessons about compassion, because I need compassion. I have learned many lessons about perseverance, because I need to persevere. I have learned to be patient. I have learned to walk in the fruit of the Spirit even when it is the last thing my body feels like doing. And, most of all, I have learned to trust God. I am definitely a better person because God has perfect timing. I struggle with chronic pain from fibromyalgia, but I live in the grace of God daily.

Do I believe God was "teaching me a lesson?" Not exactly. I have learned many things, and God knew I would, but He also knew what was best for me. He was not punishing me for my lack of faith. How do I know? I know Him.

Anyone who judges without knowing God's purposes is guilty of condemnation. Love encourages a brother or sister who is sick to keep trusting God, and commits to praying while God completes what He is doing.

The Apostle Paul put it like this when he had a thorn in the flesh. We do not know exactly what his thorn in the flesh was, but we do know he had a serious problem with his eyesight. Paul said,

"For this thing I besought the Lord thrice, that it might depart from me. And he said unto me, My grace is sufficient for thee: for my strength is made perfect in weakness. Most gladly therefore I take pleasure in infirmities, in reproaches, in necessities, in persecutions, in distresses for Christ's sake: for when I am weak, then am I strong." (II Corinthians 12:8-10)

Vines remains planted at the foot of the cross. They cannot live without the true vine. Jesus said, "Only believe." (Mark 5:36kjv)

Living vines are permanently tied to the Cross.
Dead vines are uprooted and burned.

Freedom from the Law
of Sin and Death

"Every branch in Me that does not bear fruit, He takes away;
and every branch that bears fruit, He prunes it,
that it may bear more fruit. You are already clean,
because of the word I have spoken to you."
John 15:2-3

The root of the vine is fixed, and its growth is ever deeper, but the branches are free to grow abundantly in any direction. The Vinedresser knows which branches will bear good fruit. There are fruiting branches and fruitless branches. Pruning away the non-fruiting branches provides more nourishment for the fruiting branches so they can produce good fruit. When Christ fulfilled the Law, He pruned away a fruitless system that did not produce the fruit of righteousness.

"Therefore, my brethren, you also were made to die to the Law through the body of Christ, so that you might be joined to another, to Him who was raised from the dead, in order that we might bear fruit for God. For while we were in the flesh, the sinful passions, which were aroused by the Law, were at work in the members of our body to bear fruit for death. But now we have been released from the Law, having died to that by which we were bound, so that we serve in newness of the Spirit and not in oldness of the letter." Romans 7:4-6

After a lengthy debate during the council of Jerusalem (Acts Chapter 15), the Apostle Paul decided it would be best to *ask, (not require for righteousness),* the Gentiles to do four things: avoid foods contaminated by idols, fornication, things that are strangled, and blood. Three of these relate to the worship of idols and the fourth, fornication, was rampant amongst Gentiles. Paul did not attach any of these to proof of righteousness, but rather indulged the weakness of the Jews who wanted to place the Gentiles in bondage to the law Christ fulfilled. In Romans Chapter 14 Paul explains:

"Therefore let us not judge one another anymore, but rather determine this--not to put an obstacle or a stumbling block in a brother's way. I know and am convinced in the Lord Jesus that nothing is unclean in itself; but to him who thinks anything to be unclean, to him it is unclean. For if because of food your brother is hurt, you are no longer walking according to love. Do not destroy with your food him for whom Christ died. Therefore do not let what is for you a good thing be spoken of as evil; for the kingdom of God is not eating and drinking, but righteousness and peace and joy in the Holy Spirit."

God prunes. He wants us to abandon any practice that is fruitless (I Timothy 1:5-11). Today, the most fundamental of all Christian doctrines is under attack, and many Christians are deceived by this terrible heresy. It is an evil and fruitless heresy taught in the guise of obedience to God. This heresy comes primarily through the Hebrew Roots Movement, the First Fruits of Zion Movement, and the Sacred Name Movement. These three cults have been around for more than ten years, and now have far-reaching effects. Going back under Judaic Law is a fruitless denial of Christ. Christians, whether Messianic or Gentile, are not, and never have been required to keep the Law.

There are 613 Judaic Laws listed in the Old Testament. There are also countless Laws that Jews are required to obey based on Rabbinic tradition. The food laws are a good example. The Old Testament lists some, but not all of them. For example, Kosher Law (food laws) forbids the eating of meat and dairy at the same time. The original law in the Old Testament stated that the meat of a kid (young goat) could not be boiled in its mother's milk (Exodus 23:19 and Exodus 34:26). That has evolved into a Law that forbids eating meat and dairy during the same meal. It also requires two sets of pots and pan to avoid contamination, and separate refrigerators for these products. In other words, the original Law has become more complex. This greater complexity makes it even more impossible to keep the whole Law perfectly. The Law written in Leviticus and Deuteronomy was impossible to keep in the first place, and now it is even more difficult. Sin is revealed by the disobedience of man, because He cannot keep the Law. (Romans Chapters 5 and 6)

Modern day Jews have loopholes so they can do what they want, and still obey the Law. On the Sabbath, riding an elevator is forbidden because pushing the number buttons is operating machinery. So, all elevators stop at every floor. Striking a match is work. On the Sabbath there are gas fed candles in the hotel lobbies so people can light their cigarettes without striking a match. In the time of Christ, it was unlawful to walk long distances, because it is work. So, there is a bench periodically. The traveller sits on the bench for a few minutes. Then, having technically obeyed law, the traveller can continue on his way. Such practices are not obedience to the law. They are an end run around the law. It is hypocrisy.

Repeat: God in His mercy and grace never did, and still does not require Christians to keep the Judaic Law, and Jewish believers are released from obedience to Judaic Law. God has made both groups a single group – Christians. (Ephesians 2:15-16). Christ fulfilled the Law. Yes, the Law still exists, and unsaved Jews still attempt to keep it. Christians cannot to go back under a yoke of slavery. Christ has now written His law on our hearts (James 2:12).

"For if I rebuild what I have once destroyed, I prove myself to be a transgressor. For through the Law I died to the Law, so that I might live to God. I have been crucified with Christ; and it is no longer I who live, but Christ lives in Me; and the life which I now live in the flesh I live by faith in the Son of God, who loved me and gave Himself up for me. I do not nullify the grace of God, for if righteousness comes through the Law, then Christ died needlessly." Galatians 2:18-21

"For Christ is the end of the law for righteousness to everyone that believeth." Romans 10:4kjv

The Bible addresses this issue directly in the book of Galatians. The following scriptures also reveal the truth of the matter:

> Matthew 5:17-46, Acts 13:38-39, Acts 15:1-12, Romans 8:3-4, Romans 10:4, Galatians 3:10-14, Philippians 3:7-11, Colossians 2:15-23, I Timothy 4:1-5, Hebrews 8:6-13, Hebrews 10:28-31, II Corinthians 3:12-18

We have a choice. We can allow Him to prune our lives, and cut away all dependence on law-keeping, or we can attempt to be righteous by our own effort through obedience to man-made rules.

Jesus says He will never leave or forsake us, and in fact, He offers every opportunity for each of us to walk with Him, and then spend all of eternity with Him. When we walk with Jesus, we continue to remain at His side. If there is a fork in the road, we take the fork He takes. Otherwise, we walk away from Him and go our own way by the asserting of our own self-will (Galatians 5:18-23).

We cannot ignore the role of the Holy Spirit in our lives. He is the revealer of all truth, our comforter, and the one who changes us into the image of Christ. Living by the Spirit –*walking in the Spirit* - is an essential part of our Christian experience. It is so important that the Apostle Paul tells us that living based on the Law will sever one from Christ. Falling from grace is a serious matter.

"You have been severed from Christ, you who are seeking to be justified by law; you have fallen from grace." Galatians 5:4

If you are tempted by deceivers, *choose to stay free* in the Holy Spirit. Study His word, and the Holy Spirit will guide you.

We have only one thing to offer Him:
fruit that remains.

Grafted into Christ

"Abide in Me, and I in you.
As the branch cannot bear fruit of itself,
unless it abides in the vine, so neither can you,
unless you abide in Me."
John 15:4

Grafting is the joining of two separate plants so they become one plant using a common rootstock. In the natural realm, a graft can be *compatible*, but does not have to be *identical*, to the parent plant into which the graft is placed. Here is an example using apple and pear: The *rootstock*, an apple tree sapling onto which the pear is grafted, is a branchless stem with a root.

A short piece of pear branch, called a *scion*, (SIGH-un), is the graft. It is a branch with one bud. A slit is made near the top of the *rootstock*. The rootstock and scion are joined by inserting the scion into the slit between the woody bark and the soft center of the rootstock.

Ointment seals the graft. It is wrapped, and left until the wound heals. The two become one plant. The large scar produced at the point of the graft is the only evidence of a graft. This tree will produce pears, even though the root is that of an apple tree.

This kind of *compatible* graft is not possible with God. He does not accept *compatible* grafts. The graft must be *identical* so the fruit produced by the plant is *identical* to that produced by the root. What does this mean in a vineyard?

"Therefore we are buried with him by baptism into death: that like as Christ was raised up from the dead by the glory of the Father, even so we also should walk in newness of life. For if we have been planted together in the likeness of his death, we shall be also in the likeness of his resurrection: Knowing this, that our old man is crucified with him, that the body of sin might be destroyed, that henceforth we should not serve sin. For he that is dead is freed from sin." Romans 6:4-7 kjv

Christ is the rootstock, or vine, into which we are grafted. When we come to Christ, God cuts us off from our old life, and our own dead works. We are grafted into the holy root of God. Without this identical graft, we remain dead in our sins.

"...and if the root be holy, the branches are also." Romans 11:16b

The heart of every sinner, by faith, becomes an identical match with the heart of God in this union. The Holy Spirit cuts through the hard, protective, woody bark to the soft layer beneath. God binds us together with Himself, and seals us from the world with the oil of anointing in the Holy Spirit. We are bound together with Christ. When we are grafted into Christ, a miraculous change takes place – we become identical to Him, by faith. The scar that remains is the evidence that we are not our own. We owe our very existence to God alone because compatible is not *the same as* identical.

God grafts, plants, waters and watches. In our lives, others may plant and water, but only God causes growth. We steadfastly persevere *in* Christ. (I Corinthians Chapter 3, Ephesians 4:15)

"For you have need of endurance, so that when you have done the will of God, you may receive what was promised." Hebrews 10:36

That small *scion* has one small bud, but within that bud is everything needed for the new growth of the graft. As it is with the vine, our unique giftedness is contained within this bud. In the beginning, He usually strips away all but one small part of our natural ability. In the same way, newly planted young vines are pruned to eliminate excess growth. God wants us to yield everything in our lives to Him before we branch out in a world filled with opportunities for good works.

A small graft with one little bud looks like nothing. No one can see the new life yet, but it is there. As the days lengthen, and the weather warms in the spring, the bud swells. That little bud grows into a long branch with many new buds. The graft has succeeded!

"For in Him we live, and move, and have our being;..."
Acts 17:28a kjv

and without Him...?

Fruit That Remains

"Behold, the days are coming,"
declares the LORD,
"when the plowman will overtake the reaper
and the treader of grapes him who sows seed;
When the mountains will drip sweet wine,
and all the hills will be dissolved.
Also I will restore
the captivity of My people Israel,
and they will rebuild the ruined cities
and live in them.
They will also plant vineyards
and drink their wine,
and make gardens
and eat their fruit."

Amos 9:13-14

Planting in God's Vineyard

"I am the vine, you are the branches;
he who abides in Me, and I in him,
he bears much fruit;
apart from Me you can do nothing."
John 15:5

There was a very large field behind the house where my family lived in Livermore, California. My husband and I often walked a path at the edge of that field. Prairie dogs scurried from hill to hill while cattle grazed nearby. Wild rabbits hopped away quickly as we approached, and hawks soared overhead looking for field mice. The natural beauty of our surroundings gave us an opportunity to reflect on the awesome creative abilities of God as we talked over our day.

Every fall, the owner cut and bailed the hay growing in that field. Afterward, only stubble remained. Then, when the winter rains came, water sat on the surface of the pastureland. In the spring, the hay stubble rotted, and it began to stink.

In the early spring, the farmer brought in a large machine called a disc plow. He used it to till under the rotten stubble, and "rip" through the hardpan that kept sitting water from filtering through the soil. He tilled again, and added various amendments to the soil before he distributed seed for a new crop of hay.

Along the edges of the path where we walked, a narrow band of soil remained unplowed. As the weather became warmer, the water evaporated from the surface of this untilled ground. As the ground dried up, it became deeply cracked. Then, during the hottest part of the summer, a thick white crust of alkaline salt appeared. This ground grew nothing. Any seed that attempted to sprout would be deformed and burnt on the edges. The foliage twisted and died in the summer heat. The bases of the wooden fence posts rotted because of the salt. Only the tilled areas of the field grew a good crop of hay.

This is a reminder that there is abundant life whenever God tills deeply in the field of my life. Deep tilling turns the ground of a person's life upside down. "Ripping" is painful. The Holy Spirit brings deep conviction. The saved and the newly saved experience this kind of deep tilling in the heart. The grievous pain of sin wells up and there is emotional upheaval in the soul. God tills so He can plant in good soil.

Deep genuine repentance brings peace when God tills. Only at this point in a person's life will the root be able to grow deep and yield the peaceable fruit of righteousness.

"For ground that drinks the rain which often falls upon it and brings forth vegetation useful to those for whose sake it is also tilled, receives a blessing from God; but if it yields thorns and thistles, it is worthless and close to being cursed, and it ends up being burned." Hebrews 6: 7-8

Only after the stinking stubble of the past is put under can new life come. In God's vineyard, vines are never planted in unprepared soil. Many programs of evangelism have tried to bring people into the Body of Christ in a "seeker friendly" way; that is, planting without tilling. People who are planted without deep tilling appear to be strong and healthy, but when the harsh circumstances of life come, they fall away because they have not grown a deep root.

"The one on whom seed was sown on the rocky places, this is the man who hears the word and receives it with joy; yet he has no firm root in himself, but is only temporary, and when affliction or persecution arises because of the word, immediately he falls away." Matthew 13:20-21

Pruning, uprooting, tilling the ground, and then replanting correctly may save these vines. God, in His great mercy, is the final judge, but He has already judged the world's inhabitants in His son. His mercy extends continually to those who fail in their attempts to follow Christ with their whole heart, but for those who know the truth and refuse to follow, there comes a frightful day of judgment.

Anyone who comprehends the truth, but refuses to allow God's tilling sins. We must be a light in this world. Deep tilling brings freedom from sin.

> "A man shall not be established
> by wickedness:
> but the root of the righteous
> shall not be moved."

Proverbs 12:3 kjv

Seeds

"And the seed
whose fruit is righteousness
is sown in peace
by those who make peace."
James 3:18

In every grape there are three seeds. Each seed contains the reproducible life of the plant. This is a perfect picture of our triune God.

"For you have been born again not of seed which is perishable but imperishable, *that is*, through the living and abiding word of God." I Peter 1:23

When planted, these seeds produce a plant *identical* to the original. Every plant has its own characteristics for growth, but each one contains the same foundational structure as the original. This is what happens when we receive the life of Christ through His death and resurrection. An ecumenical system, or mixture of belief systems, is not acceptable. Christianity has a foundational system called *doctrine* that must remain intact. The Bible is our foundation, and unless that remains inviolate, the truth is lost.

"Can a fig tree, by brethren, produce olives, or a vine produce figs? Neither can salt water produce fresh. Who among you is wise and understanding? Let him show by his good behavior his deeds in the gentleness of wisdom." James 3:12-13

When the body of Christ embraces unrepentant individuals, and tells them they are part of the body, it is planting the seeds of tares that produce failure. Christ accepts people as they are when they come to Him for salvation, but God expects those who come to Him to change when the Holy Spirit reveals the truth to them. Planting seeds of truth in the lives of people is the responsibility of every Christian. We do it lovingly, but honestly. We hope the seeds we plant will bear the fruit of righteousness.

When lies are planted instead of the truth, seeds of evil grow. The Bible calls these tares (weeds). They will eventually be torn out of the place where they are planted and thrown away (Matthew 13:25-40).

Do we say nothing, and wait until the final harvest, when tares are growing in the body of Christ? No. We confront; not with anger, but with the truth. We take our stand, and we do not back down. When we confront it is not judgmental, because God Himself has already judged the sins of the flesh. We are repeating what He says about sin and false doctrine.

To avoid confusion: Jesus did tell a parable about wheat and tares growing together. He said to allow them to grow together, and God would judge between them at the time of the final harvest. This parable does not apply to the body of Christ. It applies to the secular world in which the body of Christ must live

Loving one another is not cheap. It often requires us to sacrifice more than we think we have (or want) to give. It takes time, study in the scriptures, prayer, and genuine friendship. Seeds grow slowly, but the right seed planted at the right time will grow into a fruitful vine. How willing are you to serve with a grateful heart and plant seeds even if you do not see immediate growth? Do you enjoy helping people? That's what this journey is about: giving ourselves to others – even when our motives are misunderstood. We plant. We plant. We plant... (Matthew 13:4-9). Is this what Jesus did?

As a body, it is time to stop using clichés from the past, and think through the pat answers that seem so cheap when people are deeply wounded. It is said, "We put everything *under* the blood," but, this is not what the Bible tells us about the blood of Christ. Those who live based on an Old Testament system of law put sin 'under the blood,' but whatever is merely *covered* is not *removed*. When Christ died and rose from the dead, He *sanctified* us *(set us apart unto Himself)* once and for all through the offering of His blood. The shedding of His blood *removed* our sin. *Those washed by His blood are cleansed of all sin and set free* (Hebrews Chapter 10).

Remember, our entire fight is to *stay free*. We choose to stay free by confessing our sin, and dying to our own selfish desires.

"...putting aside all malice and all guile and hypocrisy and envy and all slander, like newborn babes, long for the pure milk of the word, that by it you may grow in respect to salvation." I Peter 2:1-2

"Oh give thanks unto the LORD,
for He is good:
for His mercy endureth for ever."

Psalm 107:1 kjv

Jo Hinds

"But my God shall supply
all your need
according to His riches in glory
by Christ Jesus."

Philippians 4:19 kjv

Rambling Vines - the First Season

"By this is My Father glorified,
that you bear much fruit,
and so prove to be My disciples."
John 15:8

During the first year, the Vinedresser allows the young vines to *ramble (grow freely without any restraint.)* They ramble because they have little strength of their own. Their branches are pliable and easily damaged. They bear no useable fruit, but they do establish a taproot. Young vines are shaded and protected under the branches of mature vines planted on either side of them. It is two or three years before young vines grow tall enough to tie in the position they will hold for the rest of their lives. During that time, careful pruning shapes the vines so they will bear good fruit when they are mature.

In the church, leadership positions are thrust upon novices. A novice is a *rambler.* Zeal and intellectual knowledge appeal to carnal men, but God's word is plain:

"(but if a man know not how to manage his own house, how shall he take care of the church of God?); not a novice, lest being lifted up with pride he fall into the condemnation of the devil." I Timothy 3:5-6 kjv

The ability to teach the crucified life comes from lessons learned over time. God calls mature workers to equip the saints,

"for the perfecting of the saints for the work of the ministry, for the edifying of the body of Christ till we all come in the unity of the faith, and of the knowledge of the Son of God unto a perfect man, unto the measure of the stature of the fullness of Christ: that we henceforth be no more children, tossed to and fro, and carried about with every wind of doctrine, by the sleight of men, and cunning craftiness, whereby they lie in wait to deceive;" Ephesians 4:12-14 kjv

Age does not necessarily equate with maturity, but a new convert in Christ never does. A vine must first grow up in Christ (Ephesians 4:23-24).

"My brethren, count it all joy when ye fall into divers temptations;
Knowing this, that the trying of your faith worketh patience.
But let patience have her perfect work,
that ye may be perfect and entire, wanting nothing."

James 1:2-4 kjv

The Second Season

"And since we have gifts that differ
according to the grace given us,
let each exercise them accordingly…"
Romans 12:6a

Rambling vines cannot carry their own weight. Immature clusters of grapes are removed from ramblers so all the growth goes into the vine. Ramblers do not start growing fruit that matures until at least the third season. Mature fruit is large, and contains sweet juice that has a full-bodied flavor. God's workers wait patiently. To help young vines mature, vineyard workers cut away most of the vigorous branches at the top of the vine to direct growth *inward* and *downward* so the vine will be strong and tall, and the root will grow deep into the ground. During the next few seasons larger quantities of grape clusters appear.

Vineyard workers watch to see which stem is the strongest, straightest, and tallest. When it reaches the height of the crossbar, it is tied permanently to the upright post. All the other rambling branches are cut away. This main stem hardens off (becomes woody and strong like a tree trunk). It takes several seasons for the stem to gain the strength needed to carry the heavy weight of vigorous branches.

The spiritual life of every believer begins the same way: *tied to the cross*. Disciples learn to drink from the deep well of God during the early seasons of their walk with the Lord. If they are not tied to the cross, they will *ramble* until they are fully grounded in the Word of God, or they fall away (I Timothy 4:6-8).

"These things command and teach."

I Timothy 4:11 kjv

47

Hedged Vines

"Create in me a clean heart,
O God;
and renew a right spirit within me.
Cast me not away
from Thy presence; and take not thy
Holy Spirit from me.
Restore to me the joy of thy salvation;
and uphold me with thy free spirit.
Then, I will teach transgressors
Thy ways;
and sinners will be converted
unto thee."

Psalm 51:10-13 kjv

Training Methods

"Just as the Father has loved Me,
I have also loved you;
abide in My love."
John 15:9

The names of two predominate methods of training are *cane* training and *arc-cane* training. Both methods require pliable young vines to take the shape of the cross permanently. The *climate* where the vines are grown determines the best method to use. This is also true for every fellowship of believers. Each group develops a climate or culture.

Using the *cane training method* means cutting away all but two branches at the top of the upright stem. One branch is tied to the left of the vine, and the other is tied to the right. All new growth will come from the buds on these two horizontal canes. This type of cane training requires skilled labor. It is more work than other methods, but the vines will be less sensitive to early spring freezes, and they will produce larger fruit. This method is used for table grapes (the ones we buy at the grocery store).

The *arc-cane training* method is the bundling together of several canes to the left and several to the right on the cross-member. This allows more fruit bearing buds per vine and higher yields. There is also a more consistent crop level, and more uniform vine growth. Grapes grown for winemaking are grown this way. Smaller grapes, but higher yields produce more juice. This method also produces more grape skins. The skins add flavor and color to wine.

Some congregations train disciples individually. This is like the *cane* training method. Others train disciples in a school of ministries or home fellowship groups bundling people together like the *arc* training method. In either case, elders teach novices. Both methods are acceptable. It is the *culture* in which the training methods happen that makes all the difference.

One (or both) of these methods must be used to grow grapes. Vines will not tend themselves. Allowing vines to ramble does not produce good fruit. The leadership of every congregation is responsible for training disciples in a Biblical climate without mixture (no strange or false doctrine).

Leadership is also responsible for removing any cultural peculiarities that are contrary to godly living. Church elders must discipline, (exhort, rebuke and teach in the love of Christ), those who willfully sin against God. Only Godly training produces mature vines.

"Shepherd the flock of God among you,
exercising oversight not under compulsion,
but voluntarily, according to the will of God;
and not for sordid gain, but with eagerness;
nor yet as lording it over those allotted to your charge,
but proving to be examples to the flock."

I Peter 5:2

Propagation

"And they, continuing daily with one accord in the temple,
and breaking bread from house to house
did eat their meat with gladness and singleness of heart,
praising God, and having favour with all the people.
And the Lord added to the church daily
such as should be saved."
Acts 2:46-47

Mature vines produce branches used for *propagation* by *air and ground layering*. When *air layering* is used, a vineyard worker packs damp peat moss (supplemented with nutrients) around a joint on a strong branch. Heavy mil plastic tied around the bundle seals in the moisture. In time, roots grow out of the joint into the peat moss. The bundle and a section of the branch are cut away for planting. This method produces an *identical* plant. Mentoring programs work in this way.

The *ground layering* method also uses a strong branch. A long branch is pulled down onto the ground so a joint of the branch can be placed in a shallow hole. Two crossed sticks hold the branch down while a mound of soil buries the joint completely. A stone placed on top of the mound keeps the joint buried until a new root grows.

A worker cuts the newly rooted vine away from the branch out of which it grew. This vine is also *identical* to its parent. By either method, burial of the parent plant occurs to create an identical offspring. Paul's words to the Ephesians tell us to,

"For we who live are constantly being delivered over to death for Jesus' sake, that the life of Jesus also may be manifested in our mortal flesh."
II Corinthians 4:11-12

"But may it never be that I should boast, except in the cross of our

Lord Jesus Christ, through which the world has been crucified to me, and I to the world." Galatians 6:14

> "Humble yourselves, therefore, under the mighty hand of God,
> that He may exalt you at the proper time."

> I Peter 5:6

Hedging - Cutting Away Wild Growth

"If you keep My commandments,
you will abide in My love;
just as I have kept My Father's commandments,
and abide in His love."
John 15:10

Wild branches are *hedged*. Hedging is the cutting away of any branch that cannot be bent and tied to the cross-member and is not fruit bearing. Unhedged branches tangle themselves up between the rows. In some congregations, there is complete disarray. Individuals meddle, gossip, backbite, and slander others. A framework of order cannot be neglected in any large group of individuals. Having a framework of order is not the same as controlling everything happening in the group. People must be free to do every good thing, but they cannot interfere with the basic tenets of body life. We respect our elders, and maintain a culture of kindness. Members of the body whose arrogance does not leave room for others to go about the Lord's work without interference need to be *hedged*, because their actions are fruitless and chaotic.

I have attended women's groups where several members formed a clique to exclude anyone the clique thought to be beneath their status. This kind of behavior must be stopped. Many young Pastors and their wives are fearful that these controllers will leave a small congregation when they are called to account. Let them leave, and do not fear! *Hedging* wild branches allows healthy plants to produce good fruit.

Vines grow *tendrils*. These are long curlicue fingers. They twine around other branches and hold fast. They are unyielding and demanding. They strangle the movement of the branches around them. They hold on so tightly they are impossible to remove. *Tendrils* are cut away when non-fruit bearing branches are hedged. If not, they become unyielding, and workers cannot walk through the rows to tend to the needs of the vines.

Like *tendrils*, what we are unwilling to yield often interferes with the sovereign plan of God for our lives. Clinging to people as a source of happiness, or by man-pleasing brings bondage. This kind of unhealthy neediness stifles the life of a believer. *Hedging* removes the cling-fast tendrils and sets the vine free. After removing the tendrils, the vine can stand independently. *Hedging* and removing *tendrils* is a necessary part of discipleship in any church, because wild growth prevents the vine from focusing on its most important task - fruit bearing. We cannot entangle ourselves in the carnal world's methods or practices (Hebrews 12:1).

Oh, the groaning that takes place in our soul when we say we are willing to submit to His hedging, but refuse to allow it. Dying-to-self means yielding everything. Do you hear His still small voice speaking to you about hedging? What will you allow Him to do? This is why we wait upon Him. *Waiting upon Him is not idleness.* Hedging seems painful because we measure success and failure by how much pain we feel, but God measures based on the fruit produced in difficult circumstances.

What is your response to circumstances you do not like? Do you press in or shrink back? God *hedges* because He loves you, and wants you to bear good fruit. He wants you to produce an abundance of good fruit. Do you have a sense of inner peace in the Holy Spirit no matter what happens? Allow Him to *hedge* your life and your lifestyle.

Rest in Him

The Third Season

"These things I have spoken to you,
that My joy may be in you,
and that your joy may be made full."
John 15:11

At the beginning of the third season, the stem has reached the height of the cross-member. The workers select two branches for horizontal training across the top of the cross-member. The vine no longer rambles, and it is no longer allowed to entangle itself in the growth of other vines.

When the vine begins to produce good fruit, and every succeeding season, the Vinedresser expects crops of good fruit. Only mature vines produce fruit used to make new wine. Once the vine begins to produce mature fruit, only what the Vinedresser desires is acceptable. In the beginning, we take up our cross in selfless service to God because Christ has,

"…canceled out the certificate of debt consisting of decrees against us and which was hostile to us; and He has taken it out of the way, having nailed it to the cross." Colossians 2:14

After becoming conformed to the cross, we serve Him because we love Him. Many mature older Christians think retirement means they may retire from active service for the Lord, but this is a mistake. We are clearly told that older women should teach younger ones, and mature men become mentors to novices.

"Older women likewise are to be reverent in their behavior, not malicious gossips, nor enslaved to much wine, teaching what is good, so they may encourage the young women to love their husbands, to love their children, to be sensible, pure, workers at home, kind, being subject to their own husbands, so that the word of God will not be dishonored." Titus 2:3-5

It is also a mistake for Pastors to think older members of the congregation have nothing to offer. Age brings experience – both good and bad. Older Christians have gained wisdom with age through their life experiences. They are a rich source of knowledge in any congregation.

"You younger men, likewise, be subject to your elders, and all of you, clothe yourselves with humility toward one another, for God is opposed to the proud, but gives grace to the humble." I Peter 5:5

Preserve the unity of the Holy Spirit

"Come unto me,
all ye that labor and are heavy laden,
And I will give you rest.
Take my yoke upon you,
and learn from Me;
For I am meek and lowly in heart:
and
You ye shall find rest unto your souls.
For My yoke is easy,
and My burden is light."

Matthew 11:28-30 kjv

Conformed To Christ

"This is My commandment,
that you love one another,
just as I have loved you."
John 15:12

Eventually, tender young branches conform to the shape of the cross. Workers must not force the vines to conform beyond their ability to bend. Severely bending young vines causes them to snap. Many branches break away because the pressures of conformity are too great.

The law revealed the futility of attempting to obtain perfection through our own efforts. Only conformity to the cross by subjecting oneself to the discipline of the Lord leads to a *change of heart*. Conformity in the flesh eventually becomes a burden that is impossible to carry. Many Christians fall away because they try so hard to do everything right, and find themselves failing again and again. Either they come to the end of themselves or they quit trying. A root of bitterness often begins to grow when the believer cannot meet the expectations of those around him.

"Before faith came, we were kept under the law, shut up unto the faith which should afterwards be revealed. Wherefore the law was our schoolmaster to bring us unto Christ, that we might be justified by faith. But after that faith is come, we are no longer under a schoolmaster." Galatians 3:23-25 kjv

The natural growth pattern that causes untrained branches to grow straight up exalted in pride, and out to the sides distracted by the pull of worldly things, are pruned away by the Lord. What remains are the branches trained by the discipline of the Lord. When tied to the cross, you can no longer choose which way you want to go. You are now committed to living a life shaped by the cross. Your life is hidden in Christ. While we do not like correction, yielding brings peace. Any time you are without peace, ask the Holy Spirit what is out of order. You may not be doing anything wrong, but something is not in order with what God wants (Hebrews 12:11).

All disciples must be willing to bend in humility, and accept training by God's restraining hand. As we yield, we gain strength waiting upon Him, and conformity *to Him* becomes our permanent stature.

"…Now may our Lord Jesus Christ Himself and God our Father, who has loved us and given us eternal comfort and good hope by grace, comfort and strengthen your hearts in every good work and word."
II Thessalonians 2:16-17

Unhedged Vine

"The LORD is righteous in all his ways,
And Holy in all his works.
The LORD is nigh unto all them that call upon him,
to all that call upon him in truth.
He will fulfill the desire of them that fear him:
He also will hear their cry
and will save them.
The LORD preserveth all them that love him:
But all the wicked, will he destroy."

Psalm 145:17-20 kjv

Growing Fruit that Remains

"Greater love has no one than this,
that one lay down his life for his friends."
John 15:13

Many people think fruit is the outcome of ministry to others, and that Jesus is referring to *good works* when He says He wants our fruit to remain. Some people think fruit is what we *do* for someone else – it is a gift we give them - one that we hope will have a profound and lasting effect on their lives. *This is not the fruit Jesus is talking about in John chapter 15.*

Have you ever seen a vine bear fruit on the vine planted next to it, or one planted miles away in another vineyard? Have you ever seen any fruit-bearing plant, shrub or tree bear its fruit on another plant, shrub or tree? Where does fruit grow? Every vine bears its fruit *on its own branches.* The Master's fruit is not the result of what we do for others, but what we allow God to do in us. The Vinedresser picks this fruit from the vines in His vineyard for His exclusive use. The fruit of the Spirit in our lives bears witness of Him.

Only
through witnessing my
transformed life
are those around me changed.

"You are my friends,
if you do what I command you.
No longer do I call you slaves,
for the slave does not know
what his master is doing;
but, I have called you friends,
for all things that I have heard
from My Father
I have made known to you."

John 15:14-15

Pruning

"You did not choose Me, but I chose you, and appointed you,
that you should go and bear fruit, and that your fruit should remain,
that whatever you ask of the Father in My name, He may give to you."
John 15:16

Near the end of the long growing season, workers *hedge* the branches to expose clusters of nearly ripe grapes to bright sunlight. It is simple. The greater the light, the faster the fruit matures. At the end of each fruit-bearing season, the Vinedresser prepares the vines for a season of rest during which they wait for a new season of fruitfulness. The specific needs of each type of vine determine how it is pruned. The deep cut of pruning comes just as the long winter is almost past.

While the vines are still dormant in the spring, workers cut the fruit-bearing branches back to three buds, and completely remove all non-fruiting branches. This seems extreme, but it is necessary for the production of top quality fruit. Then, there is a time of waiting. The surge of warm spring weather brings new foliage and newly set fruit.

Our lives as Christians consist of this: We are grafted into Him, and we remain deeply rooted in Him. We yield to His Holy Spirit; grow good fruit, and wait for Him to pick it. Then, we trust Him to *hedge* errant growth, prepare us for winter dormancy, and allow spring pruning. Should we resist the pruning process? Who among us can knowingly resist Him without regret? The place of *abiding* is a place of yielding and rest. The vine is active, but it is also at peace with its place in the world. A dead branch is evident even to those who know nothing about vineyards – the works of the flesh are evident to all.

Resisting the pruning of the Lord brings *burnout*. Burnout is anxiety, stress, and confusion from work done in the flesh. The work itself may be productive and helpful in the community, but it may not be part of God's plan for *your* life. God's plan, no matter how exhausting physically, comes with peace, and the desire to see the project through to the end. *Burnout, frustration, and anxiety* are evident when one wants a long-enduring task to end. It does not matter what name we use; the result is the same. A worker without peace is working in the flesh.

> Comprehend the will of the Lord.
> He wants you to live in peace.

Pruning When the Time and Season are Right

"This I command you,
that you love one another"
John 15:17

Pruning too late, when the sap has already started to run, causes excessive bleeding. Young vines rarely recover when subjected to indiscriminate pruning, or *over cropping*. If too many of the fruiting branches are removed, the vine suffers.

Over cropping causes mature vines to set fruit late and produce less fruit. When the fruit has less time to mature, the flavor is less intense. Severely pruned mature vines are less susceptible to damage than tender young vines, because the older growth of mature vines has *hardened off*, but all vines are susceptible to death if treated severely.

Vines are pruned so they will bear better quality fruit, and for no other reason. If workers prune for any other reason, they are not following the Vinedresser's instructions. Workers who prune in God's vineyard are,

"...pure, peaceable, gentle, reasonable, full of mercy and good fruits, unwavering and without hypocrisy, and the seed whose fruit is righteousness is sown in peace by those who make peace." James 3:16-17

One morning as Jesus returned to Jerusalem with his disciples He became hungry. He saw a fig tree by the road. When He found no fruit on the tree, Jesus said the tree would never again bear fruit, because it did not serve the purpose for which it was planted (Matthew 21:18-19).

In the story of the fig tree, Jesus was hungry, but there was no fruit to eat so he caused the barren tree to wither. God created each of us with a purpose. If we do not produce the fruit of righteousness in our lives, and fulfill our purpose, we will wither. Do you understand that your purpose in life is to bear fruit that remains? Shrinking back leads to destruction.

"Now the just shall live by faith: but if any man draw back, My soul shall have no pleasure in him. But we are not of them who draw back unto perdition; but of them that believe to the saving of the soul." Hebrews 10:38-39 kjv

To draw back means to shrink back. It is described as cowering in fear. Only those living out their purpose, producing the fruit of the Spirit, and *fighting to stay free until the end*, will hear the words, "Well done."

"But now being made free from sin, and become servants to God, ye have your fruit, unto holiness, and the end everlasting life." Romans 6:22 kjv

The purpose of God in giving each of us unique talents is to use them for the glory of God. Jesus told His disciples this story: He was hungry, thirsty, a stranger, naked, sick, and in prison and they had taken care of Him:

"Then shall the King say unto them on his right hand, Come, ye blessed of my Father, inherit the kingdom prepared for you from the foundation of the world: For I was an hungred, and ye gave me meat: I was thirsty, and ye gave me drink: I was a stranger, and ye took me in: Naked, and ye clothed me: I was sick, and ye visited me: I was in prison, and ye came unto me. Matthew 25:34-36 kjv

When the disciples asked when they did all these things, Jesus said,

"The King shall answer and say unto them, 'verily I say to you, inasmuch as ye have done it unto one of the least of these my brethren, ye have done it unto me.'" Matthew 25:40 kjv

"For to everyone who has, more shall be given, and he will have an abundance; but from the one who does not have, even what he does have shall be taken away." Matthew 25:29

My relationships with other people, and the use of my God-given talents, are for the glory of God alone. If I use them for any other self-serving purpose, I will wither like the fruit tree, and my talents will disappear. What did the King say about those who do something else…?

"Throw out the worthless slave into the outer darkness;
in that place there will be weeping and gnashing of teeth."

Matthew 25:30 kjv

"Who among you is
wise and understanding?
Let him show by his
good behavior
his deeds
in the gentleness
of wisdom."

James 3:13

Weeds in the Vineyard

Abiding Vines

"He has told you, O man, what is good;
and what does the LORD require of you
but to do justice, to love kindness,
and to walk humbly with your God."
Micah 6:8

Vines *abide*. They are planted firmly in God's vineyard, and they cannot be moved. They quietly produce good fruit. They worship God when His gentle breeze blows, and the sun shines. They endure.

The people who touch my life most deeply are those who *abide* in the love of Christ. They know God. My best friends teach others how to walk in the ways of the Lord. They come alongside others to encourage them. They pray secretly and in public. They refuse to give up when a friend struggles. They love beyond errors made, and they exhort the weak. They are teachable, and they ask for help. We share all things in common. We love one another.

The people who touch my life most deeply do all of this without asking for public recognition. They are filled with the joy of the Lord, and their laughter is a medicine. Spending time with them brings back lost hope, banishes discouragement, and sends all who meet them out into the world with renewed vigor for serving God. These are genuine servants of God. Do you know someone who *abides* like this?

The church is a family. It is nothing like the competitive world system. The church does not climb ladders to achieve success. *It abides.* Our focus is not on building worldly kingdoms.

"For we know that if the earthly tent which is our house is torn down we have a building from God, a house not made with hands, eternal in the heavens." II Corinthians 5:1 (Read II Corinthians Chapter 5 for the context.)

"For the love of Christ controls us, having concluded this, that one died for all, therefore all died; and He died for all, so that they who live might no longer live for themselves, but for Him who died and rose again on their behalf." II Corinthians 5:14-15

No one person, or council of people, ranks higher than anyone else in the family. Why do so many individuals want their leaders to be corporate CEO's who are treated like the Hollywood elite? In the Old Testament, the people cried, "We want an earthly King. We want Saul" (Acts 13:21). God wanted to lead them, but they did not want Him to be their leader. Is that what the body of Christ is doing today?

There are Christian entertainment awards, but there are no grand televised awards for the people who volunteer to teach children, clean the church, set up and take down chairs, cook food, do the dishes, and comfort those in need. Have you ever wondered why?

It is time we take our stand, refusing to follow a worldly model of secular leadership in the body of Christ. *We can no longer afford to follow God and man at the same time.* Only if our leaders are following God alone can we follow them. You love them, but discern their ways.

"You shall walk after the LORD your God, and fear Him, keep his commandments, and obey his voice, and ye shall serve him, and cleave unto him" Deuteronomy 13:4 kjv

Many leaders in the secular corporate world separate themselves from the masses by having a suite of offices, requiring appointments, avoiding contact with their audience, and living at a financial level beyond the reach of their employees. They are unapproachable, untouchable, authoritarian, controlling, and expect *their people* to get him/her where *they* want to go. This is not abiding.

Those who abide are in the trenches fighting the good fight, learning to persevere in fellowship with others, and carrying those who are too frail to go it alone. We live, work, and survive the ravages of a secular, immoral world with the help of those around us. Every worker in God's vineyard protects the vineyard, and grooms it for fruit production. Anything else is the world's way.

"He who descended is Himself also He who ascended far above all the heavens, that He might fill all things. And He gave some as apostles, and some as prophets, and some as evangelists, and some as pastors, and teachers, *for the equipping of the saints for the work of service* to the building up of the body of Christ; until we all attain to the unity of the faith, and of the knowledge of the Son of God, to a mature man, to the measure of the stature which belongs to the fullness of Christ." Ephesians 4:10-13

Congregations that allow leaders to climb to the pinnacle of pride, put them on a pedestal, allow them to preen publicly, have the last say, and consider them wise without question, are guilty of idolatry. Living vicariously through the successful programs of our leaders is complete failure for those who do it. Each of us is called to take our stand as individual members of the whole.

For even the Son of Man did not come to be ministered unto, but to minister, and to give His life a ransom for many." Mark 10:45 kjv

Ministry is service. We are servants. If we wait for someone to wait on us, we are masters, and no longer servants. Go first. Offer to help others. Think like this: "what can I do to make the lives of those around me more comfortable?" Do you purposefully inquire about the needs of others? Do you eagerly enjoy finding out about the living conditions of your neighbors? Do they need something you can give? A servant lives to serve. Do you? I like working with a group, and turning work into an opportunity for fellowship. What do you think?

Each of us will stand as individuals before God one day. Merely attending services at a mega-church will not unlock the gates of heaven. God's first question will be: "Do you know my Son?" Then, He will look in the Lamb's book of life to see if your name is registered there. Faith in Him requires the belief that His death and resurrection are sufficient, and He won the victory – therefore, we do not chase prophets. We do not abandon our liberty. We live out our own calling – not that of an earthly master. We serve others because we love Christ. We *abide in* Christ.

"For as we have many members in one body, and all members have not the same office: so we, being many, are one body in Christ, and everyone members one of another." Romans 12:4-5 kjv

There is nothing wrong with expressing our doubts, admitting our failures, and asking for prayer to help us persevere in taking our stand at the foot of the cross and choosing to stay free. This is our fight – not one of getting free, but staying free. If you go into bondage, a choice (whether you knew it or not) was made to give away your precious freedom, and the only solution is to repent. God will then restore you to a place of complete freedom without any condemnation, and you can move forward fighting once again to stay free. This is persevering in the love of God.

Those who abide know He is with them. *He does not punish* us, but He does *discipline* us for failing in our attempts at obedience. Discipline graciously trains us in the ways of the LORD. Only those who are teachable are trainable.

He comforts us when we embarrass ourselves by making silly mistakes. He lifts us up when we must admit we are wrong. He never turns away anyone coming to Him for assurances of His love. He encourages, strengthens, shares all things, refreshes, enjoys and loves all who meet Him. This is what we do for one another.

> "But now *abideth* faith, hope, charity, these three;
> but the greatest of these is charity."
>
> I Corinthians 13:13 kjv

Dormancy

"It is God who is at work in you,
both to will and to work
for His good pleasure."
Philippians 2:13

Dormancy in winter prepares the vines for the coming season of fruitfulness. The buds on the fruiting spurs begin to swell in the spring. They sense changes in the climate. The hidden life suddenly bursts forth. What looked dead is not. What was not seen becomes plainly visible, but dormancy comes first. This is what God does in our lives.

What do you enjoy doing? Do you get up in the morning saying, "I guess I *have to* go out and have fun today...?" No. We delight in doing what gives us joy. Vines accept the seasons. They accept dormancy as part of life. They do not chafe or refuse to go dormant. They know that resting is good.

Dormancy is not idleness. Nor is it laziness. God wants us to spend time with Him. Restlessness is symptomatic of refusal to wait upon the Lord. Dormancy refreshes our souls, and prepares us for a future time of fruitfulness. It brings hope, and provides precious time to renew our commitment to abiding.

Any time you work begrudgingly, examine your motives: Why am I doing this? Perhaps your heart is not in your work because you are filling your time with busy work instead of spending time with Him. Spending time with the Lord brings rest. If you go to Him because you are not at peace, He will give you peace. Wait on Him until you are at peace.

Vines rest in the winter. When the winter ends, they grow. Vines grow because it is their nature. They grow without giving thought to what it will look like to any other vine, and they do not hesitate to do what is right – in season and out of season.

Jo Hinds

"Preach the word; be instant in season, out of season; reprove, rebuke, exhort with all longsuffering and doctrine." II Timothy 4:2 kjv

When the winters of life come remember…

God is love

"Religious" Workers

"If the world hates you, you know that it has
hated Me before it hated you.
If you were of the world, the world would love its own,
but because you are not of the world, but I chose you out of the world,
therefore, the world hates you."
John 15:18-19

A vineyard has varieties of vines producing differing kinds of grapes. Each type has a specific purpose. The head vintner (wine maker) tells the workers what is needed. If he does not do his job properly, the vineyard suffers. Workers in the vineyard treat each varietal with the care needed for fruit production. If they do not know what is best for the vines, and they do not learn good training methods, they will follow destructive growing methods. Workers need to know *why they do what they do*, not only *how to do what they are told*. Jesus said this about 'religious' leaders (Scribes and Pharisees):

"All therefore whatsoever they bid you observe, *that* observe and do; but do not ye after their works: for they say, and do not. For they bind heavy burdens and grievous to be borne, and lay *them* on men's shoulders; but they *themselves* will not move them with one of their fingers. But all their works they do for to be seen of men: they make broad their phylacteries, and enlarge the borders of their garments, And love the uppermost rooms at feasts, and the chief seats in the synagogues, And greetings in the markets, and to be called of men, Rabbi, Rabbi. But be not ye called Rabbi: for one is your Master, *even* Christ; and all ye are brethren. Matthew 23:3-9 kjv

A *hypocrite* says one thing but does another. Leaders who operate out of a *religious spirit* (a spirit that uses Biblical references and Jewish Law to deceive people), gain a following because those who follow do not test every spirit.

"Beloved, believe not every spirit, but try the spirits whether they are of God: because many false prophets are gone out into the world."

I John 4:1 kjv

One of the gifts given by the Holy Spirit is the *distinguishing of spirits* (more commonly called, *discerning of spirits*). It is through this gift that the Holy Spirit reveals the truth to us about the spirits operating around us. Pray that this gift will once again open the hearts and minds of believers all over the world to understand that not all spirits operating are from God. A *religious spirit* is cloaked in a religious form, but it does not come from God. It employs the 'wisdom of the wise' (secular logic) to deceive.

"For it is written, 'I will destroy the wisdom of the wise, and will bring to nothing the understanding of the prudent." Where is the wise? Where is the scribe? Where is the disputer of this world? Has not God made foolish the wisdom of this world?" I Corinthians 1:19-20 kjv, Isaiah 29:14 kjv

"But we preach Christ crucified, unto Jews a stumbling block, and unto the Greeks foolishness, but unto them which are the called, both Jews and Greeks, Christ the power of God and the wisdom of God."

I Corinthians 1:23-24 kjv

Jesus also talked about these religious workers when He told this parable about religious workers in God's vineyard:

"Hear another parable: There was a certain householder, which planted a vineyard, and hedged it round about, and dug a winepress in it, and built a tower, and let it out to husbandmen, and went into a far country: And when the time of the fruit drew near, he sent his servants to the husbandmen, that they might receive the fruits of it. And the husbandmen took his servants, and beat one, and killed another, and stoned another. Again, he sent other servants more than the first: and they did unto them likewise. But last of all he sent unto them his son, saying, They will reverence my son. But when the husbandmen saw the son, they said among themselves, This is the heir; come, let us kill him, and let us seize on his inheritance. And they caught him, and cast him out of the vineyard, and slew him. When the lord therefore of the vineyard cometh, what will he do unto those husbandmen? They said unto him, He will miserably destroy those wicked men, and will let out his vineyard unto other husbandmen, which shall render him the fruits in their seasons" Matthew 21:33-41 kjv

The vine-growers are stewards of God's possessions. Before He leaves workers in charge of His vineyard, He instructs them. The Bible is God's instruction book for all leaders. Those who claim to serve God as leaders in the body of Christ cannot claim ignorance when confronted for mistreating God's people in His vineyard. Any form of *discipleship* that usurps the instructions of the Lord is rebellion. What are leaders doing that usurps God's instruction?

God instructs His workers to protect the vines, feed them, give them water, hedge away rampant new growth that will not produce fruit, propagate new vines by an acceptable method, harvest the grapes to make new wine, and prune the vines while they are dormant in winter. Workers must do all of these things without bringing any glory to themselves.

Today there are countless congregations with leaders whose sole purpose is church-building – not building up the church. Shall we allow immorality within the body to avoid offending? Shall we stop preaching/teaching from the *literal* Bible to make the Bible more easily understood? Shall we stop preaching the gospel of Christ – His death and resurrection – to make Biblical living more palatable? Shall we fix our eyes upon a 'famous man' who leads a mega-congregation rather than the author and finisher of our faith who is Christ? Shall we focus on wealth, faith in our own faith rather than faith in Christ, and in the power of our own words – rather than the power of the Holy Spirit to make visible the will of God in our lives?

Arrogant men who enjoy their 'following,' and have unimaginable wealth at their disposal, believe they are successful. God does not measure success by the number of people in a congregation, in currency, or the quantity of possessions people own. This is what the apostle Paul wrote to the Corinthians church about wealth:

"For if there be first a willing mind, it is accepted according to that a man hath, and not according to that he hath not. For I mean not that other men be eased, and ye burdened: But by an equality, that at this time your abundance may be a supply for their want, that their abundance also may be a supply for your want: that there may be equality: As it is written, He that had gathered much had nothing over; and he that had gathered little had not lack."

II Corinthians 8:12-15 kjv, Exodus 16:18 kjv

God provides wealth to some people so they can supply the needs of those who are less fortunate. Giving is a gift freely given to benefit someone else not ourselves. God does not want stored riches. He does not think Pastors need paychecks like corporate heads; nor do they deserve great wealth and ease of living. He does not want us to focus on the acquisition of money as a motivation. Nor does He promise that 'pledged' money multiplies like a good investment. In fact, Paul says to give based on what you presently have – not what you do not have (which is the definition of 'pledging').

God wants us to give to those in need so no one lives in poverty. He wants those with great wealth to use it for God's glory. Vineyard workers who hoard wealth for themselves instead of training the Vinedresser's vines are *lovers of pleasure* and *impostors*. God is interested in our personal character (and integrity) rather than our worldly success.

"But if ye be led of the Spirit, ye are not under the law. Now the deeds of the flesh are manifest, which are these; Adultery, fornication, uncleanness, lasciviousness, idolatry, witchcraft, hatred, variance, emulations, wrath, strife, seditions, heresies, envyings, murders, drunkenness, revellings, and such like: of the which I tell you before, as I have also told you in time past, that they which do such things shall not inherit the kingdom of God." Galatians 5:18-21 kjv

At the end of this list, the New American Standard Bible says, *"And things like these…"* What things like these? Malice, guile, hypocrisy, filthiness, bitterness, wrath, clamor, slander, idolatry, unbelief, lust, unbridled tongue, disobedience, cursing, rebellion, murdering, empty talkers, wrangling about words, *lovers of self,* boastful, revilers, ungrateful, unloving, irreconcilable, malicious gossips, without self-control, brutal, haters of good, treacherous, conceited, lovers of pleasure rather than God, immorality, holding a form of godliness but denying its power, turning to myths, *impostors,* factious, judging with evil motives, factions, selfish ambition, jealousy adultery, arrogance, tumult, impurity, anarchy, instability, confusion, fears, disturbances… This is a collection of many works of the flesh mentioned in the New Testament. As you read your Bible, you will find more.

"…do you not know that friendship with the world is hostility toward God? Therefore whoever wishes to be a friend of the world makes himself an enemy of God." James 4:4

In every vineyard, vines grow side by side. Their branches touch each other. They share the same plot of ground. They drink the same water. They have all things in common. On the day of Pentecost: (Read Acts Chapters 1 and 2)

"They were continually devoting themselves to the apostles' teaching and to fellowship, to the breaking of bread and to prayer." Acts 2:42

"Everyone kept feeling a sense of awe; and many wonders and signs were taking place through the apostles." Acts 2:43

"And all those who had believed were together and had all things in common; and they *began* selling their property and possessions and were sharing them with all, as anyone might have need." Acts 2:44-45

"Day by day continuing with one mind in the temple, and breaking bread from house to house, they were taking their meals together with gladness and sincerity of heart, praising God and having favor with all the people. And the Lord was adding to their number day by day those who were being saved."

Acts 2:46-47

Jesus sent a helper, the Holy Spirit, to remind the vine-growers of all He had instructed them to do. Those who usurp God's authority are in grave danger. They make *themselves the owner of the vines* instead acting as God's caretaker. They *steal* God's glory.

"And whoever causes one of these little ones who believe to stumble, it would be better for him, if with a heavy mill stone hung around his neck, he had been cast into the sea." Mark 9:42

> Some who claim to know Him
> do not do what He commanded.
>
> Love speaks and lives the truth

Tendrils

Hirelings

"Remember the word that I said to you,
'A slave is not greater than his master.'
If they persecuted Me, they will also persecute you;
if they kept My word, they will keep yours also."
John 15:20

This is the definition of a *hireling*: *A temporary worker hired to do a job.* Self-interest is the hireling's primary motive for service. He wants to climb a ladder of success. He will follow without ever questioning the practices of the leader, if the reward is great enough.

These workers are the *underlings* who follow false teachings and pass it on in the body. In a vineyard, there are supervisors and hired hands. Supervisors instruct hirelings. Hirelings do not question the validity of these instructions. We are not hirelings. We are the Vinedresser's children. We have the authority to question any instruction given us, and God requires us to do so.

American pastors are usually taught that the pastor is to provide the *vision* (spiritual insight) for the body. Leaders who steal the liberty of God's people boast, "This is *my* church, and these are *my* people. *I* have a vision for them, and anyone who joins *my* church must share *my* vision." The saints are told to fulfill the leader's vision. Consequently, the people are required to work for the pastor. This is the opposite of God's instructions. The body does not work for the pastor; the pastor works for the body. The idea of a vision comes from a phrase out of the Old Testament:

"Where there is no vision, the people are unrestrained," Proverbs 29:18a

The word unrestrained is defined as, *out of control.* 'No vision' in this proverb means the people have an '*inability to see clearly.*' It does not suggest that someone else see for them. The Holy Spirit enables every individual to see clearly. It is the job of the pastor to equip the people to fulfill the vision God gives them as individuals.

The objection to each individual having a personal vision, or calling, is that there will be chaos in the body if the people are not restrained, and it is the job of the pastor to *control the body* so there will not be an outbreak of confusion. This is false. When everything is decent and orderly, the body remains in order. The Holy Spirit is fully capable of controlling the lives of people, if He is allowed to do so. The pastor and elders reprove, rebuke and exhort only when needed for personal growth, and they equip the saints to do the work of the ministry.

Is this more difficult than preparing a speech every week, and standing behind a podium for an hour or so? Yes. Is it more personal? Yes. Those who are unable or unwilling to establish personal relationships within the body cannot adequately do pastoral ministry. Those who build mega-churches cannot do this either. Mega-church congregations need to be split into many small congregations (either actually or within the congregation), and numerous small fellowship groups led by elders.

"And it shall come to pass in the last days, saith God, I will pour out my Spirit upon all flesh: and your sons and your daughters shall prophesy, and your young men shall see visions, and your old men shall dream dreams: And on my servants and on my handmaidens I will pour out in those days of my Spirit; and they shall prophesy:" Acts 2:17-18 kjv (The apostle Paul is quoting Joel 2:28-32)

"And calling them to Himself, Jesus said to them, 'You know that those who are recognized as rulers of the Gentiles lord it over them; and their great men exercise authority over them. But it is not so among you, but whoever wishes to become great among you shall be your servant; and whoever wishes to be first among you shall be slave of all." Matthew 20: 25-27

"Let not many of you become teachers, my brethren, knowing that as such we will incur a stricter judgment." James 3:1

"For though by this time you ought to be teachers, you have need again for someone to teach you the elementary principles of the oracles of God, and you have come to need milk and not solid food." Hebrews 5:12

Do you remember when the phrase, "don't touch God's anointed" began going around in the body of Christ? Leaders who embraced this meant, "Never question *my* authority." They, in essence, forbade the use of the gift *discerning of spirits*, and took captive those who followed them. We never question *God's* authority, but because men are fallible, we do test every spirit to protect our freedom in Christ.

In I Chronicles 16:22, (the scripture from which this false teaching is derived) the *context* refers to God's people, the Israelites, *in their entirety.* The statement, "do not touch My anointed ones," is part of a prayer of thanksgiving spoken by Asaph and his relatives when the ark of the covenant was placed inside a tent pitched for it by David. Psalm 105:15 repeats this same phrase with the same intent as I Chronicles 16:22. *Always check the context in scripture when you hear unusual teachings.*

We are responsible for guarding ourselves, and those around us. Evil workers who manipulate people with this false teaching use King David as an example. They cloak the deception in *religious language* when they say: "I have authority over this congregation. I am responsible for what happens, and my word is final." They allow no discussion, no accountability, and no respect for the thoughts or feelings of others.

Periodically, a heavy-handed teaching by *false prophets* has had the same effect. People lost their liberty because of this lie. They cannot come and go freely without permission from a self-appointed false prophet. Even the choice of a husband or wife needs permission from a prophet. This is bondage. When we walk in the law of liberty, we are free to come and go as we please. God asks us to use our liberty for the benefit of others; God does not permit anyone to place others in bondage. Many congregations fall prey to this deception.

In these cult-like congregations, anyone who objects is *falsely accused* of having their own agenda. When a leader defines *loyalty to himself* as proof of faithfulness, he is self-serving. Faithfulness is defined Biblically as 'filled with faith in God.' *It is a condition of the heart.* It is outwardly lived and seen, as *trustworthiness.*

Evil workers use harsh words, as well as benevolent persuasive speech, to manipulate. These leaders declare themselves accountable to all, but are accountable to no one. They are benevolent – unless provoked by words they do not want to hear. Then, they are angry. We are, indeed, to view ourselves as one with the body of Christ and say, "these are my people," when it is inclusive. However, when a leader says, "these are *my people*," boasting of ownership, he is wrong to think he has the right to possess

God's children. God is the Vinedresser. *He alone owns every vine planted in the vineyard.*

"... the Holy Spirit of promise, who is given as a pledge of our inheritance, with a view to the redemption of *God's own possession*, to the praise of His glory." Ephesians 1:13-14

"Verily, verily, I say unto you, he that entereth not by the door into the sheepfold, but climbeth up some other way, the same is a thief and a robber." John 10:1 kjv

"I am the door: by Me if any man enter in, he shall be saved, and shall go in and out, and find pasture." John 10:9 kjv

Jesus offers the freedom to come and go freely. For any worker to declare that God speaks through them alone, and the vines are required to obey their voice, *quenches* the Holy Spirit. The truth is...

"For there is one God, and one *mediator* between God and men, the man Jesus Christ." I Timothy 2:5 kjv

The Vinedresser requires workers to maintain a Godly environment. When the Vinedresser appears, He knows if the wrong spirit is hovering among the vines. He senses that the Spirit is *quenched*.

When the Spirit is quenched, He withdraws until He is allowed to once again move freely through the vineyard. When the Holy Spirit withdraws, worldly spirits fill the void. How does this happen? Did someone open the gate, or did the evil one climb over the fence while the workers were not on guard? Leaders and teachers are accountable to God for what they do, and what they teach. They must be adequately equipped to sense the presence of any spirit other than the Holy Spirit in the midst of the congregation.

"But the goal of our instruction is love from a pure heart and a good conscience and a sincere faith. For some men, straying from these things, have turned aside to fruitless discussion, want to be teachers of the Law, even though they do not understand either what they are saying or the matters about which they make confident assertions." I Timothy 1:5-7

"For the time will come when they will not endure sound doctrine; but after their own lusts, shall they heap to themselves teachers, having itching ears; and they shall turn away their ears from the truth, and shall be turned unto fables." II Timothy 4:3-4 kjv

"But false prophets also arose among the people, just as there will also be false teachers among you, who will secretly introduce destructive heresies, even denying the Master who bought them, bringing swift destruction upon themselves." II Peter 2:1 (Read II Peter Chapter 2)

In your own life, when you find your peace disturbed, or you think you are in a spiritually dry desert, it could be because the Spirit is quenched – either in your life, or the lives of some (or all) of the people with whom you fellowship. Ask the Holy Spirit to reveal the root causes. Then, pray for yourself and the brethren. Watch for an opportunity to minister with love into the situation, but do not participate in a system of error. Guard the vineyard in a godly way.

"Draw near to God, and He will draw near to you. Cleanse your hands, you sinners; and purify your hearts, you double-minded. Humble yourselves in the presence of the Lord, and He will exalt you." James 4:8,10

We learn from one another, and we defer to the gifts and callings of our brethren with the utmost respect, but we bow to no one as our king. God is sovereign in the life of every Christian. Any form of church government that steals your liberty is *cultic* in its very nature.

"For you were called to freedom, brethren; only do not turn your freedom into an opportunity for the flesh, but through love serve one another."

Galatians 5:13

The clear instructions for *every* fellowship of Christian believers are these:

Encouraging others, and helping them grow in the grace of God. Especially help those who are weary or weak from fighting the good fight.

Appreciate and highly esteem those who instruct you, and love them for their diligent work on your behalf.

Be at peace and enjoy the fellowship of the saints, and exercise patience with everyone you meet.

Never participate in any scheme that repays a wrong with vengeance, but have mercy on all.

Worship, pray, express thanksgiving, and live out God's plan for your life.

Live out your freedom in Christ through the Holy Spirit. Encourage the gifts of the Spirit to operate, and listen intently when someone speaks prophetically.

Use discernment so you will not be deceived, and you can snatch others out of the clutches of the enemy. Look at everything said and done with wisdom.

Refuse to go any way that takes you away from freedom in Christ.

Do what you know is right, and bears the fruit of the Spirit, and reject any temptation to sin. (I Thessalonians Chapter 5)

How important is it to actively live out our calling? Is it possible to live every day without thinking through what is happening around you? Christ calls us to a life that is proactive, not passive. Is attendance at a church services once a week sufficient for those who are called to love one another? You cannot sit in a chair in a church service listening to a single leader day after day, and expect genuine fellowship to occur. We must be involved in the lives of those around us. That only happens with intent. Notice in God's instructions, there is no mention of *preaching from a proof text,* or *seminars for adults that are not Biblical. Teaching from the Word of God, worship, and fellowship* is the pattern for Christian living.

"That the *communication* of thy faith may become effectual by the acknowledging of every good thing which is in you in Christ Jesus."

Philemon 1:6 kjv

Fellowship: The Greek words are *Koinonia, Metoche, Koinonos*: communion, sharing in common, partnership, a partaker or companion.

Teach: The Greek words are *Didasko and Paideuo*: to give instruction in Godly living and service; to instruct and train.

Workers who create a worldly system of regulations for body life subtly, slowly, create bondage. Vines do not flourish in such an environment. They sulk – waiting for the nourishment needed for growth. They must drink deeply from the root, which is Christ, or their thirst is not satisfied.

"Remember those who led you, who spoke the word of God to you; and *considering the result of their conduct*, imitate their faith." Hebrews 13:7

Soon, there will not be a place in the vineyard for workers who have come into the vineyard over the wall instead of through the door.

God is, indeed, opposed to the proud.

"Beware of evil workers.
...Put no confidence in the flesh"

Philippians 3:2-3

Climate

"But all these things they will do to you for My name's sake,
because they do not know the One who sent Me."
John 15:21

Vines develop to full maturity slowly. They do not like transplanting. They want to remain planted even when they are in bad soil, but moving vines is necessary if the growing conditions are inadequate to produce good fruit. Understanding the *climate or culture*, including the ground in which the vines are planted, is critical. God plants in good soil. The world plants in any soil available.

While vines are tenacious, they do not like heavy soil. Clay soils smother the roots because water cannot penetrate deep into the ground. This prevents the vines from growing a deep tap-root. Soil filled with nutrients, and a free-flowing water supply is ideal. Vines will grow in rocky soil if the water supply is constant. The body of Christ is much like this.

Every gathering of believers develops a culture or climate. Members quickly learn the unspoken social rules. The social climate sets members free to be about their Father's business, or it subtly hinders them through both expressed and unexpressed expectations, and bad programming. The kind of soil into which vineyard workers plant vines is vitally important to their future well-being.

What would happen if legalistic programs and teaching the latest religious fads were eliminated? What if preaching the Gospel in all humility – the good news about Jesus Christ, and Him crucified and risen from the dead, and what that means for godly living were the consistent message? What do you think it would look like in practice? Why do few churches teach principles of Godly living, dying-to-self, and rising in newness of life? God's workers must take their instructions from the Vinedresser to make it happen. It is time for the climate to change.

"That we henceforth be no more children, tossed to and fro, and carried about with every wind of doctrine, by the slight of men, and cunning craftiness whereby they lie in wait to deceive; but speaking the truth in love, may grow up into him in all things, which is the head, even Christ." Eph. 4:14-15 kjv

The good news is not only a spoken message. It is lives lived wholeheartedly for Christ.

It is:
Filled with the Holy Spirit
Devotion to the apostles teaching
Fellowship and breaking of bread
Prayer
Feeling a sense of awe
Experiencing signs and wonders
Being together
Having all things in common
Sharing what is owned to meet the needs of others
Continuing with one mind in the Temple
Taking meals together with gladness and sincerity of heart
Praising God and having favor with all the people

Because of these things, their numbers grew daily. Acts 2:42-46

Why
was the Lord
adding to their number
day by day…?

Aged Vine

Destructive Lice

"If I had not come and spoken to them, they would not have sin,
but now they have no excuse for their sin. He who hates Me hates My
Father also. If I had not done among them the works which no one
else did, they would not have sin; but now they have both seen and
hated Me and My Father as well. But they have done this to fulfill the
word that is written in their Law,' They hated Me without a cause."
John 15:22-25

The Phylloxera Root Louse can destroy an entire vineyard before it
is discovered. These microscopic lice do their destructive work hidden in
the soil. They secretly kill the roots of non-resistant vines. By the time the
vines wither, it is too late to save them. Insidious small things will destroy
a body of believers in the same way.

Within the body of Christ, worldliness, indifference, lack of genuine
love and tolerating sin are as destructive as a louse in a vineyard. Those
resistant to the destruction leave, and what remains is a fully corrupt
religious system. God hates sin.

Yes, He loves saints saved by grace, but those who yield to temptation
thinking it makes no difference to God are mistaken, and it will cost them
dearly when they stand before Him someday. No one can claim to love God and
sin willfully. God forgives, but He also disciplines. Those whose hearts harden,
and refuse to change, will incur His wrath. While love covers a multitude of
sin, it does not sweep it under the carpet, or pretend it is acceptable.

"Above all, keep fervent in your love for one another, because love
covers a multitude of sins. Be hospitable to one another without complaint.
As each one has received a *special* gift, employ it in serving one another, as
good stewards of the manifold grace of God." I Peter 4:8-10

Love *covers sin* by dealing with it privately instead of exposing it
through backbiting, gossip, and/or shunning. Indifference toward the

presence of sin within the body silently destroys the body through broken relationships, divisive cliques, greed, a desire for personal power, and unwillingness to yield when the Holy Spirit brings conviction. Sin cannot be ignored. Clearly, Jesus says those who sin willfully cannot claim to know God. It is a powerful, even unnerving, charge against God's elect.

"And by this we know that we have come to know Him, if we keep His commandments. The one who says, I have come to know Him, and does not keep His commandments, is a liar, and the truth is not in him; but whoever keeps His word, in him the love of God has truly been perfected." I John 2:3-5a

This tiny Phylloxera Root Louse creeps in subtly, and once it takes hold it is pervasive. Take for example various methods for emotional healing that have swept through the body. There was a teaching in the 1990's that said we are not really *born again* until we are cleansed through a tedious process of renouncing by name countless demonic spirits. Needless to say, thousands of people went through this heretical program before it was renounced by those who endorsed it in the first place. Why did so many Christians finish a program that denies the most basic tenant of Christianity – the *doctrine* of salvation?

"For by grace are ye saved through faith; and not that of yourselves: it is the gift of God: not of works, lest any man should boast." Ephesians 2:8-9 kjv

Programs such as recovery of lost memories, healing the inner child, co-dependency, and variations of new age meditation convince the participants to pray a certain way, heal oneself by self-talk, and change the past by self-deception to acquire the freedom Jesus *has already won* for us at the cross.

We pray for *physical healing* through private and corporate prayer (James 5:14). We *deliver the oppressed and possessed* through deliverance, and we *comfort* those who mourn the death of loved ones, but today's churches want to *heal the works of the flesh* instead of *removing them*.

Anger is the root of the vast majority of issues involving emotional pain (anger from disappointment, betrayal, divorce, and various offenses). God gave us only one solution for emotional healing: faith in the death and resurrection of Christ. It is that simple. We die to our past, and past hurts, and we rise in newness of life.

"…except a corn of wheat falls into the ground and dies, it abideth alone: but if it die, it bringeth forth much fruit." John 12:24 kjv

One can receive relief from emotionally painful situations by using methods other than "dying daily" as the Apostle Paul says. However, using methods other than what God offers *rejects the power of the cross*.

Fellowship is ordinary Biblical counsel. We discuss the situation with other believers in a Godly manner, and ask for prayer focused on the victory of Christ. False programs do not focus on Christ. Instead they focus on solutions accomplished by the person in pain: Find out what hurt you in the past, take these steps..., quote these scriptures, pray this way. Dying to self is not mentioned as part of the solution.

"Confess your faults one to another, and pray one for another, that ye may be healed. The effectual fervent prayer of a righteous man availeth much." James 5:16 kjv

"Therefore consider the members of your earthly body as dead to immorality, impurity, passion, evil desire, and greed, which amounts to idolatry. For it is because of these things that the wrath of God will come upon the sons of disobedience, and in them you also once walked, when you were living in them. But now you also, put them aside: anger, wrath, malice, slander, and abusive speech from your mouth." Colossians 3:5-8

Answer this question: For which issues in life are *emotional healing* most often requested? Is it those with a root in *passion?* Passion is one of the works of the flesh defined as: *An intense desire to fix, change, lash out against, or get rid of emotional anger or hurt?*

Read again the solution offered in Colossians 3:1-8. Every *false method has a spiritual cloak* (the deception is hidden by a *religious spirit*), but these methods (or programs) do not teach denial of one*self,* humility before God, giving the situation to Him, or refusing to take it back once it has been turned over to God. Methods other than death-to-self are false. They do not bring lasting freedom. *ONLY through the cross is transformation possible.*

Remember: You may get relief from your pain through other methods, *but you will not be changed into the image of Christ.* Read once again what Paul wrote to the Philippian church:

"...that I may know him, and the power of his resurrection, and the fellowship of his sufferings, being made conformable unto his death; if by any means I might attain unto the resurrection of the dead." Philippians 3:10-11 kjv

"...*being conformed to His death;*" Sanctified Christians choose to allow the Holy Spirit to intervene on their behalf rather than taking matters into their own hands. We choose to be "dead to sin" (those we commit, and those committed against us). This is *crucifying the flesh*. We are united in the power of the risen Lord, and we are conformed to His death when we follow His example:

"Have this same attitude in yourselves which was also in Christ Jesus, who, although He existed in the form of God, did not regard equality with God a thing to be grasped, but emptied Himself, taking the form of a bond-servant, and being found in appearance as a man, He humbled Himself by becoming obedient to the point of death, even death on a cross" Philippians 2:5-8

This is the anchor for our souls: We have only one means to solve our earthly problems, that is Jesus Christ and Him crucified and risen from the dead.

Do you want deliverance from evil? Your deliverance has already come through the shedding of Christ's blood on the cross. Paul says,

"Do you not know that when you present yourselves to someone as slaves for obedience, you are slaves of the one whom you obey, whether of sin resulting in death, or of obedience resulting in righteousness?" Romans 6:16

"I am amazed that you are so quickly deserting Him who called you by the grace of Christ, for a different gospel; which is really not another; only there are some who are disturbing you, and want to distort the gospel of Christ." Galatians 1:5-6

The *gospel* is a gospel of peace. Is your peace disturbed by emotional issues? Then, do not be deceived by earthly solutions. Paul put it this way:

"But even though we, or an angel from heaven, should preach to you a gospel contrary to that which we have preached to you, let him be accursed." Galatians 1:8-9

Accursed. That is a harsh word! Paul is clearly stating that there is only one way to be saved from a 'sting of death.' Any other way nullifies the death of Christ.

"O DEATH, WHERE IS YOUR VICTORY? O DEATH, WHERE IS YOUR STING? The sting of death is sin, and the power of sin is the law; but thanks be to God, who gives the victory through our Lord Jesus Christ." I Corinthians 15:55, Isaiah 25:8

There is one more form of destruction working its way through the roots of the vineyard. It creeps in to destroy the vineyard out in the open when it has the opportunity. It is unafraid of sleeping workers. Like the Phylloxera Root Louse, it destroys without detection:

There are numerous books called Bibles, but many of them are not a Bible. To be a Bible, a book must be an *inspired literal translation* of the *Scripture*. Inspired means the Word is anointed by the Holy Spirit to contain the power of God. The Holy Spirit, the power of God, reveals the truth through the Word of God. The Bible tells us:

"All *Scripture* is given by inspiration of God, and profitable for doctrine, for reproof, for correction, for instruction in righteousness: that the man of God may be perfect, thoroughly furnished unto all good works."

II Timothy 3:16-17 kjv

A *literal translation* of the Word of God comes from the oldest known original texts. Some of the original texts were found within the last two hundred years. Information about Old Testament texts is less known because of their age, but scholars who compare very old texts with more recent ones find only minor differences. The texts used for literal translations are reliable.

The <u>New American Standard Bible</u> (NASB) is a *literal translation* from ancient texts. It is *inspired literal scripture*. This means it is a word-for-word translation of the original texts with consideration given for the grammatical structure of the original languages.

The <u>King James Bible,</u> which is also called the <u>Authorized Version,</u> is an *inspired literal scripture* translation, but the English used in it is now archaic, and the meanings of many words have changed since 1611. However, the basic doctrines are accurate, and it is a *literal translation*.

The <u>New King James</u> is an updated version of the <u>King James Bible</u>. It has solved many of the language issues by substituting current words for archaic ones. It is an excellent choice for those used to reading the <u>King James</u>. It is a *literal translation*.

The <u>New International Version</u> (NIV) is part *literal* and part *literary*. What does this mean? Some of this book is translated word-for-word, and some of it is written based on *what the translators think it means*. The author or authors have *paraphrased* many passages.

Beware: what a translator *thinks* the text means may be different from what it actually says and means. Paraphrased passages are not the *inspired* Word of God unless they are closely tied to the *literal* translation.

A carefully paraphrased Bible is acceptable as a study guide, but it is always necessary to compare a *paraphrase* to a *literal* translation. A paraphrase is not recommended by this author as a primary Bible for study.

Finally, there are many *paraphrased* books that are not the Word of God (nor are they Bibles). This destructive louse, if permitted to work undiscovered, could destroy the body of Christ. Here is one example: The Message is a fully *paraphrased* book. It is entirely uninspired, and is *not a* Bible. This book proves how dangerous it is to trust an uninspired book as a source for truth.

Romans 15:13 in The New American Standard Bible reads:

"Now may the God of hope fill you with all joy and peace in believing, that you may abound in hope by the power of the Holy Spirit."

Romans 15:13 in The Message reads:

"Oh! May the God of *green* hope fill you up with joy, fill you up with peace, so that your believing lives filled with the life-giving *energy* of the Holy Spirit, will brim over with hope!"

Who is the *God of green* hope? It is a *new age diety* derived from various sources: Druid tradition, earth and nature worship, and the *green man* worshipped by wiccans, masons, and Satanists. Green hope, based on gnostic teachings, is heretical.

The words *energy* of the Holy Spirit is a new age substitution for *power* of the Holy Spirit. There are so many new age and occult references in The Message it is impossible to excuse them as paraphrased from the original texts. This book eliminates completely the names *Lord Jesus* and *Lord Jesus Christ*. Numerous important verses are left out entirely. It is a deceptive new age lie posing as scripture.

Recommendation: If you know someone who uses this book instead of a Bible, tell him/her to destroy it. If you own one, destroy it so no one else is deceived by its writings. Christians must guard their hearts and minds. Discern the truth and stay free.

Good fruit is borne on disease free vines.
The others die

The Lord is the Spirit

"When the Helper comes, whom I will send to you from the Father,
that is the Spirit of truth, who proceeds from the Father,
He will bear witness of Me, and you will bear witness also,
because you have been with Me from the beginning."
John 15:26-27

Jesus died to set humanity free from the law of sin and death, but sin remains without genuine repentance. Without the Holy Spirit, there is no means for heart transformation. The Holy Spirit was *with* many people before Christ rose from the dead, but He was not resident *in* them. Before the crucifixion, Jesus told His disciples,

"...I will ask the Father, and He will give you another Helper, that He may be with you forever; that is the Spirit of truth, whom the world cannot receive, because it does not behold Him or know Him, but you know Him because He abides with you, and will be in you." John 14: 16-17

"Nevertheless I tell you the truth, it is expedient for you that I go away; for if I go not away, the Comforter will not come unto you; but if I depart, I will send him to you." John 16:7 kjv

The feasts of Israel prophetically proclaimed the coming of the Jewish Messiah Jesus Christ. There are four spring feasts: *Passover, Unleavened bread, First fruits and Pentecost.* The first three are celebrated in succession. Pentecost comes fifty days after the Feast of first fruits. The death and resurrection of Jesus was the fulfillment of these prophetic feasts (Read Leviticus 23).

The crucifixion occurred on the Feast of Passover. The day following Passover, on the first day of the week, the Feast of Unleavened Bread begins. This feast lasts seven days. It was the evening of the first day of the week (Sunday) when Jesus appeared to the disciples for the first time. The Feast of First Fruits is on the second day of the Feast of Unleavened Bread.

Christ, who is our Passover lamb, cleansed us from all leaven (leaven is sin). When He rose from the dead, He fulfilled the Feast of first Fruits, and He made a way for us to become new creatures.

"Clean out the old leaven, that you may be a new lump, just as you are in fact unleavened. For Christ our Passover also has been sacrificed. Let us therefore celebrate the feast, not with old leaven, nor with the leaven of and wickedness, but with the unleavened bread of sincerity and truth."

I Corinthians 5:7

"But now Christ has been raised from the dead, the first fruits of those who are asleep. But each in his own order: *Christ the first fruits*, after that those who are Christ's at His coming," I Corinthians 15:20,23

"In the exercise of His will He brought us forth by the word of truth, so that we might be, as it were, the *first fruits* among His creatures." James 1:18, Leviticus 23:17

The Feast of Pentecost fulfills the prophetic message in Joel 2:28-29.

Jesus appeared to His disciples after he rose from the dead on the first day of the *Feast of Unleavened Bread.*

"Then said Jesus to them again, Peace be unto you: as my Father hath sent me, even so send I you. And when he had said this, he breathed on them, and saith to them, 'Receive ye the Holy Ghost." John 20:21-22 kjv

This was their *born-again* experience. Jesus appeared to them on other occasions over the next forty days. On the day He ascended into heaven, He gathered them together and commanded them to remain in Jerusalem, and wait. When Jesus told His disciples to wait for the Holy Spirit to come, did He remember that He had previously breathed on His disciples and told them to receive the Holy Spirit? Yes, He did!

"…for John baptized with water, but ye shall be baptized with the Holy Ghost not many days hence." Acts 1:5 kjv

The Feast of Pentecost is the only feast when the people wave two *leavened* loaves of bread before the Lord. These leavened loaves represent those saved by grace. Jesus wanted His disciples to receive *the power of the Holy Spirit* so they could fulfill the great commission, and have the power to live godly lives. Jesus wanted the Holy Spirit, who was *with* them, to be *in* them. He told them they would be baptized with power to serve God. This sequence of events tells us that the baptism of the Holy Spirit is a separate experience from receiving the Holy Spirit at the time of salvation.

After Jesus ascended into heaven, the disciples returned to Jerusalem to wait. About one hundred and twenty people, including Mary the mother of Jesus, were in the upper room when they experienced the fulfillment of the Feast of Pentecost.

"And suddenly there came from heaven a noise like a violent rushing wind, and it filled the whole house where they were sitting. And there appeared to them tongues as of fire distributing themselves, and they rested on each one of them. And they were all *filled* with the Holy Spirit, and began to speak with other tongues, as the Spirit was giving them utterance." Acts 2:2-4

"Be filled with the Holy Spirit" is a command from Jesus. We cannot live without the guidance and power of the Holy Spirit. We can learn spiritual things intellectually; we can live a moral life with a good reputation in our community through our obedience to the law; we can to teach the Word of God with powerful results, because God honors His Word, but eternal transformation does not occur. God cannot honor the person who looks morally pure, but has produced this result through self-righteousness.

The Holy Spirit is the third *person* in the trinity of God. Shall we reject Him? A large segment of the body of Christ wants the Holy Spirit to be *with them*, but *fears* asking Him to *fill them* with the power to serve Him. Fear is not from God. What is the worst that can happen if you ask the Holy Spirit to fill you with the power to serve God?

"For everyone who asks receives, and he who seeks finds, and to him who knocks it shall be opened. Or what man is there among you, when his son shall ask form for a loaf, will give him a stone. If you then, being evil, know how to give good gifts to your children, how much more shall your Father who is in heaven give what is good to those who ask Him!" Matthew 7:8-9,11

"Now, the Lord is that Spirit; and where the Spirit of the Lord is, there is liberty." II Corinthians 3:17 kjv

Remember:
Jesus breathed on His disciples, and said,
"Receive ye the Holy Spirit,"
John 20:22 kjv

See a follow-up study of the *Baptism in the Holy Spirit* in the Appendix.

APPENDIX

Peace and Rest

Use the following outline for further study

Rest: Greek *Anapausis*
Cessation, refreshment, A harmonious working of all faculties and affections: cessation from my own works
Sabbath = Rest (Matthew 11:28-29)
Peace: Hebrew *"Shalom"*
The word shalom primarily means 'wholeness," welfare, completeness, soundness, at ease, contentment, reconciled, peace
The same word is used in all these instances:
Joshua 8:31 as "unhewn" (still complete)
Ruth 2:12 "full"
Nehemiah 6:15 "finished"
Isaiah 26:3 "made perfect"
'God of Peace' = God's character
Knowing God's character is a critical part of having a relationship with Him
Romans 15:33; 16:20, Philippians 4:9, Hebrews 13:20 Compare with I Corinthians 14:33; II Corinthians 13:11
In the Old Testament, the word *peace* is often rendered *Soteria* = Salvation
II Thessalonians 3:16-the title of God, "Lord of Peace," Psalm 4:8, Psalm 147:14, Proverbs 3:17, 16:7
To be at peace, one must be reconciled to God:
Isaiah 26:3 "The steadfast of mind Thou wilt keep in *perfect peace* (Shalom 'salvation'), because he trusts in Thee."
Hebrews 12:11 "All discipline for the moment seems not to be joyful, but sorrowful; yet to those who have been trained by it, afterwards it yields the peaceful fruit of righteousness."
James 3:17-19 "The wisdom from above is first pure, then peaceable, gentle, reasonable, full of mercy and good fruits, unwavering, without

hypocrisy. And the seed whose fruit is righteousness is sown in peace by those who make peace."

How do we acquire and maintain these two?

Is it possible to turn away from Christ through self-deception?

Are Peace and Rest, the same thing?

Is it possible to have one without the other?

What are the root causes for lack of spiritual peace?

What are the root causes for lack of spiritual rest?

"Self" – The Root of Selfishness and Pride

Sums up the natural law

Ephesians 5:29 - "No one ever hates his own flesh, but nourishes and cherishes it."

God's desire for us:

Philippians 2:3-5, Galatians 2:20, I John 1:9

Teachings on Self in the world and in the Church today:

One must first forgive and love one-self (God playing)

We are told to think *more highly* of ourselves instead of learning humility

Sometimes we are inexplicably told to forgive God! Has He sinned?

Co-dependency (*Caring too much about others* instead of caring more for ourselves)

Demonic Root problems: Pride and Low *Self*-Esteem

Pride is thinking too much of one*self,* and acting upon that belief in an *outward* manner. Pride demands attention.

Low self-esteem is thinking too little of one-self outwardly, but believing everyone else must provide constant attention to one's emotional needs. Low *self*-esteem is constantly focusing on one*self* and seeking attention for emotion needs. Low *self*-esteem constantly seeks proof of value from others instead of from God, and it begs for personal attention.

Low *self*-esteem is the antithesis of faith: it does not profess faith that Jesus won the victory at the cross. Instead it says, "I am not free, and I see no way to get free from my emotional burdens." The only solution for low *self*-esteem is repentance, and choosing to believe that Jesus set oneself free at the cross. Then, NEVER giving up your liberty again. The root of low self-esteem is pride turned *inward*. Galatians 6:3

Manifestations of low *self*-esteem

Looking inward. It is self-centered/ self-loving

Comparing oneself with others

Lying to oneself and others – self-deception

Desire for recognition: Accomplishments and status – begging for affirmation

"I want." Insisting things be done one's own way – even if another way is not sinful

Driven by fears

Holding on to past hurts, and using them to get personal attention

Manipulating others by helping, but with the secret motivation of approval for oneself.

Manifestations of Pride and the works of the flesh:

Selfish ambition (desiring power over others)

Bossy – likes to take charge, but wants someone else to do the work.

Jealous, Hypocritical, Accusatory, inwardly ashamed because of guilt, Fault-finding, Bitter, angry when confronted, gossip/tearing others down, controlling/threatening (if you don't do what I ask, I will…), victimizing - lashing out with accusations that diminish the value of others), Feeling ripped off or hurt when one is overlooked, defending one's own actions even when wrong, unwillingness to ask for help - a self-sufficient spirit, stubborn - not teachable, vain - overly concerned with appearance, beauty, looks, and clothes, pretentious: Putting on a public show that belies private behavior, blaming – not responsible for one's own behavior, unwilling to risk getting close to others, hiding faults, and character flaws from others rather than admitting them, refusing to ask for forgiveness from others – even when clearly wrong, self-justifying/rationalizing, trusting in oneself instead of God, unable to rejoice when others succeed.

What is pride?

Pride is exalting of self. It is self-protecting. Pride is committed to self-interests before committing to anyone else. It is building up oneself in one's own eyes and in the eyes of others. Pride is an excessive belief in one's superiority, worth, merit. Pride is a root cause of many sins. It is the means used by the natural, fleshly man in his attempts to gain power.

What does the Word of God say about pride?
All of the following verses are from the King James Version:

Proverbs 8:13 "The fear of the Lord is to hate evil: pride, and arrogancy, and the evil way, and the froward mouth, do I hate."

Proverbs 11:2 "When pride cometh, then cometh shame, but with the lowly is wisdom."

Proverbs 16:5 "Everyone that is proud in heart is an abomination to the LORD: though hand join in hand, he shall not be unpunished."

Proverbs 16:18 "Pride goeth before destruction, and a haughty spirit before a fall."

Proverbs 29:23 "A man's pride shall bring him low, but honour shall uphold the humble in spirit."

I Peter 5:5-6 " Likewise, ye younger, submit yourselves unto the elder. Yea, all of you be subject one to another, and be clothed with humility: for God resisteth the proud, and giveth grace to the humble. Humble yourselves therefore under the mighty hand of God, that He may exalt you in due time."

What are the consequences of pride?
What do we do about pride? What do these passages teach us?
Matthew 5:5-9 "Beatitudes"
Philippians 2:1-9
James 4:6-10

Humility is having an accurate view of yourself. We are created with dignity in the image of God. God values us so much He died for us. We are now children of God and heirs with Christ. We also need to recognize that God gives everything we have and are to us. We were created for His purposes not our own. Our main purpose in life is to glorify God. We need to see God in all His greatness, power and holiness. We need to also have an honest and accurate view of our sin. Proverbs 15:1-2, 22:4, Romans 12:3, 12:16

Self-Examination:
What actions develop humility?

1. Dying to Self: To really pursue holiness requires that we take action. Any actions we take are taken in the power of, and under the direction of the Holy Spirit. We do not rely on our own strength. It is the painful and effective discipline of rooting out and becoming dead to sin in all of its forms.

2. Romans 8:12-13 "So then, brethren, we are under obligation, not to the flesh, to live according to the flesh - for if you are living according to the flesh, you must die; but if by the Spirit you are putting to death the deeds of the flesh, you will live."

3. Colossians 3:5,9-10 "Put to death, therefore, whatever remains of your earthly nature: sexual immorality, impurity, lust evil desires and greed, which is idolatry." First we need to know our enemy. Sin is deeply rooted in our nature. **Galatians 5:17 & Romans 7:19-20 & I Peter 2:11.** Sin is at war with us, it seeks our ruin; and the only way to preserve ourselves is to fight back. Our objective is to put sin to death. He calls us to take the initiative against sin. This is a lifelong process. Sin never completely dies in this world no matter how weak it grows.

None of us is superior. Titles prove nothing. Only Christ in me, is the hope of glory. We are united with the risen and living Christ. He gave us a new life, a new heart, a new nature. Our inner nature delights in God. The Holy Spirit dealt a death blow to sin. God tells us that sin no longer has dominion over us. No matter how stubborn or deeply entrenched our sinful habits, sin's reign has ended and sustained pressure cannot fail to uproot it. Sin's power is broken. The Holy Spirit now indwells the believer. He is 'at work in you, both to will and to work for His good pleasure.' When the Christian fights sins, he opposes a dethroned and debilitated foe. We go into battle in the power and strength of the Holy Spirit of God. Read Romans Chapter 6

By what means do we put sin to death? Christ won this victory at the cross. We live it out in our daily lives.

Pursue and grow in your relationship with God. The more we nourish and feed our new nature, the less we focus on the lusts of the flesh. Then, we will be able to stop sin's attempts at regaining control of our hearts. We feed the new nature with the Word, prayer, worship, witnessing, and obedience. We can also practice and develop the qualities that are the most opposite of the sin we want to rid ourselves of and destroy. What will you do to feed your new man?

We need to be ruthless in starving sin of all that feeds it. To expect God to kill the lust in us while we still expose ourselves to temptation is crazy. We have a disturbing tendency to flirt with temptation, even trying to gratify our sinful desires without sinning. What we need to do is to do everything possible to avoid feeding our lustful desires. We need to value self-control above self-gratification. How have you been feeding your sinful nature? What steps do you need to take to starve your old sinful nature?

Confession and repentance. We need to remain sensitive to our sin by disciplining ourselves to confess and repent of sin as soon as we sin. True repentance involves a resolve not to sin again. It means going in the opposite direction and practicing the virtues most directly opposed to the sin from which you are turning.

Read Psalm 51 for a model of true repentance. Incomplete repentance is characterized by remorse, self-reproach or sorrow for sin generated by fear of punishment or guilt without a desire or resolve to forsake sinning.

Have you truly repented, or are you satisfied with feeling a little better because your sin out in the open?

True repentance commits to NEVER committing the same sin again, and only with the help of the Holy Spirit is that possible.

Is it possible to stumble before getting it right? Absolutely! But, God looks at the heart, and he honors the commitment to remain dead to sin, and alive in Him.

Pray. "...you do not have, because you do not ask." James 4:2

Jesus told the disciples to "watch and pray" so they would not enter into temptation.

Assignment: Memorize the scriptures that you found most helpful.

Salvation and Freedom in Christ

Use this outline for further study

Walking in the *Law of Liberty:* Read James 1:25

What does it mean to live by faith?

What is unbelief?

How do the answers to these questions determine the direction our lives?

What did Christ do for us?

Ephesians 2:8-10 "For by grace you have been saved through faith; and that not of yourselves, it is the gift of God; not as a result of works, that no one should boast. For we are His workmanship, created in Christ Jesus for good works, which God prepared beforehand, that we should walk in them."

KEY: *You* walk in them

Read: I Corinthians 2: 2-15, Romans Chapter 6

Read: Colossians 2:6-15

v. 6 walk in Him

v.7 established in faith and overflowing in gratitude

v. 8 see to it (you do it)

v. 9-10 *you have been made complete*

v. 11 removal of the flesh

v. 12 you were buried with Him, and raised with Him through faith in the working of God (do you believe what this says?). This is what water baptism represents.

v. 13 *while you were dead in trespasses you were made alive in Him*

v. 14 He cancelled out the certificate of death, and nailed it to the cross.

This is our position of FAITH. We have faith in His victory. We do not put faith in some*thing*, we put our faith in some*one*.

Why do those who profess to believe that Christ has set us free, still go to seminars that claim *taking a seminar* will set you free. This way of thinking is what James describes as "double minded. James 1: 5-7

What does faith require? 1Timothy 6: 12-13

We must fight the good fight of faith

When Christ sets us free, we are free, and our position of faith tells us that *we are no longer fighting to get free, we are fighting the good fight to stay free.*

Fight with weapons of warfare in the power of the Holy Spirit

II Corinthians 10: 3-4 *"Pulling down strongholds"* (The Greek says in some translations, 'fortresses') Read Hebrews 10:11-23.

v. 14 He has *perfected* for all time those who are sanctified!

Are we perfect? No! So we must believe that Jesus won this victory, *by faith*. When we see any imperfection in ourselves, we fight the good fight – choosing to do what Christ wants us to do, and we allow the Holy Spirit to 'perfect' us. We press forward toward the goal. Philippians 3:14

Let us hold fast the confession of our faith.

YOU DO IT! Hold fast!

Galatians 5:1, 13-26

"It was for freedom that Christ set us free; therefore, keep standing firm and do not be subject again to a yoke of slavery."

KEY: Galatians 6:14 "May it never be that I should boast, except in the cross of our Lord Jesus Christ, through which *the world has been crucified to me, and I to the world."*

What does it mean – the world has already been crucified to me? How did this happen? It is only possible to believe this by faith. You declare yourself dead to anything in the carnal world or the spiritual world that has a hold on you, and then if it tries to come back, you refuse to let it come back to steal your freedom. If you are not free, ask God to forgive your unbelief, and set you free once again. Then, and begin to walk once again in the liberty Christ won for you at the Cross.

Galatians 5:24 "Those who belong to Christ Jesus have crucified the flesh with its passions and desires."

Hold fast! (You do it! Do not let go of the liberty for which Jesus gave His life)

I Corinthians 10:13 Jesus has given us a way of escape (Repent, Crucify the flesh, go back to a position of complete freedom in Christ, walk by faith)

What is your responsibility before God in this?

Read: I Peter 2: 16-25 Especially note vs. 19-20, Romans 6: 5-7

"For if we have become united with Him in the likeness of His death, certainly we shall be also in the likeness of His resurrection. Knowing this, that our old self was crucified with Him, that our body of sin might be done away with, that we should no longer be slaves to sin; for he who has died is freed from sin." (My sin or those committed against me.)

Are you free from sin? Was your old self crucified with Him? Are you free, or are you a slave to sin?

What is the position of faith? What must you do to stay free? (Refuse to believe anything has a hold on you)

Romans 12: 21 "Do not be overcome by evil, but overcome evil with good"

Romans 8: 5-12 The mind set on the flesh is hostile toward God

Hebrews 11: 6 "Without faith it is impossible to please Him."

When you pray to ask God to set you free from something, is this a position of faith? Why or why not?

Jesus already set you free when He died on the Cross. Does He have to die again to set you free?

Our responsibility before God:

Ephesians 4: 21-24 "Be renewed in the spirit of your mind." "Put on the new self." YOU DO IT!

Hebrews 4: 2 "For indeed we have good news preached to us, just as they also, but the word they heard did not profit them, because it was not united by faith in those who heard."

Hebrews 4: 6 ..."those who formerly had good news preached to them fail to enter His rest because of disobedience."

Hebrews 4: 10 "For the one who has entered His rest has himself also rested from his works, as God did from His." We are free from our own sins and free from the effect of the sins of others because we are crucified, or dead, to the sins of this world *by faith*

What does this mean? Stop struggling to "get free" and believe that Jesus has already set you free! Trust Him to accomplish what you don't see. Declare yourself free, and don't go back. Fight to stay free.

II Corinthians 10: 3-5 "For though we walk in the flesh, we do not war according to the flesh. For the weapons of our warfare are not of the flesh, but divinely powerful for the destruction of strongholds. (THINGS THAT HAVE A STRONG HOLD ON YOU) We are destroying speculations and every lofty thing raised up against the knowledge of God, and we are taking every thought captive to the obedience of Christ."

There are many Old Testament scriptures that lead us to the Cross, and what Jesus accomplished when He was willing to shed His blood on the cross. When you read the Old Testament, watch for these prophetic statements.

Living a selfless life:
Galatians 6: 1-10, 14 Bear One Another's Burdens

The Holy Spirit in the New Testament
Use this outline for further study

Create a Bible chain so you can teach others. Beginning At Matthew 28:16 write Mark 1:7-11 in the margin. At Mark 1:7, write Mark 3:29. At Mark 3:29, write Mark 16:15-18, etc. All you need to remember is Matthew 28:16-20, and you can teach anyone about the Holy Spirit.

Matthew 28:16-20	The power of the Holy Spirit raised Jesus from the dead
Mark 1:7-11	*Jesus was baptized by the Holy Spirit*
Mark 3:29	Blaspheming the Holy Spirit – the only eternal sin
Mark 16:15-18	*Signs accompany those who believe in Jesus*
Luke 11:9-13 (v. 13)	Who is baptized in the Holy Spirit?
John 7:37-39	*Why?*
John 14:16-17	Helps, reveals truth, gives power for service, and to live a godly life. Third person in the trinity
John 15:26	*From the Father, called our Helper, witness of Christ*
John 16:7-15	Brings conviction of sin, righteousness and judgment
John 17:19	*We are set apart (sanctified) in the Truth*
John 20:19-22 (v. 22)	Jesus said, "Receive ye the Holy Spirit."
Acts 1:5-8	*He asked His disciples to wait for the Holy Spirit*
Acts 2:1-4	Came on the day of Pentecost, with fire and power

Acts 2:32	*Fulfillment of God's promise*
Acts 2:38-39, 42	Repentance, fellowship in the Spirit
Acts 4:31	*Baptized in the Holy Spirit more than once*
Acts 5:29-32	Holy Spirit is a witness of God
Acts 8:12-19	*A free gift from God received by asking for it before or after water baptism*
Acts 10:28	Household of Cornelius
Acts 10:42-48	*Men and women, young and old*
Acts 11:14-18	A baptism of power for all believers
Acts 19:1-7	*Different from water baptism, and salvation*
I Corinthians 2:12-16	Holy Spirit gives the liberty of God to believers
I Corinthians 3:8-17	*Salvation is the foundation*
I Corinthians 4:20	It is the power of God
I Corinthians 6:11,17,19	*Washing, sanctification, justification*
I Corinthians 12:1-31	The gifts given to the body of Christ by the Holy Spirit
I Corinthians 14:15	*Pray and sing with the Spirit. Interpret to edify the Body*
I Corinthians 14:18	Apostle Paul spoke in tongues
Galatians 5:13-26	*Walking in the Holy Spirit contrasted with the fleshly walk*
Galatians 6:7-8	Sowing and reaping in the spiritual realm
Ephesians 6:18	*Pray and persevere in the Holy Spirit*
Philippians 1:9	Love must abound in real knowledge and discernment
I Thessalonians 5:19-23	*Pattern of living in the Holy Spirit*

II Timothy 1:7	God gives a Spirit of power, love, and a sound mind
Jude 1:20	*Build up your holy faith, praying in the Holy Spirit*

Jesus wants His disciples to receive the Holy Spirit.
What do you want?

The Spring Feasts of Israel and Their Prophetic Fulfillment

Use this outline for further study

There are four spring feasts mandated by the LORD in the Old Testament. All of these feasts were prophetic. All of them were fulfilled by Christ. Read the following scriptures. Also, read the additional references to gain further understanding on the importance of the Feasts of Israel. The fall feasts of Israel, as prophesied, have yet to be fulfilled.

Passover: Exodus 12:1-14
                               I Corinthians 5:7-8

Unleavened Bread: Exodus 12:15-20, Isaiah 53:5
                               Romans 1:11-15

First Fruits: Exodus 23:16, Leviticus 23:9-23, Numbers 28:26
                               Romans 8:23, James 1:18

Pentecost: Joel 2:28-32
                               Acts Chapters 1-2

Additional references:

Levitt, Zola. *The Seven Feasts of Israel*. Dallas, TX: ZOLA, 1979
Moody, Valerie. *Feasts of Adonai*. Lubbock, TX: Gibora Productions, 2010
Slemming, Charles W. *Thus Shalt Thou Serve*. Fort Washington, PA: ChristianLiterature Crusade, 1988

Printed in the United States
By Bookmasters